The Direct Selling Revolution

The Direct Selling
Revolution

Dominique Xardel

BLACKWELL
Business

First published 1993

Blackwell Publishers
238 Main Street
Cambridge, Massachusetts 02142
USA

108 Cowley Road
Oxford OX4 1JF
UK

Library of Congress Cataloguing-in-Publication Data
A CIP record for this book is available from the Library of Congress.

British Library Cataloguing in Publication Data
A CIP record for this book is available from the British Library.

ISBN 0-631-192298

Typeset in 13 on 15 Garamond by TecSet Ltd, Wallington, Surrey
Printed in Great Britain by Biddles Ltd, Guildford & King's Lynn
This book is printed on acid-free paper

This book is dedicated to the two million independent Amway distributors and to Amway's people-oriented managers throughout the world in the hope that it will help them help others achieve their goals.

Contents

Contents

Preface

I am not a businessman or a journalist. I am an educator. Formerly the Director of ESSEC, a leading graduate business school in Paris, and copy editor of the French edition of the *Harvard Business Review*, my mission is to learn how different corporations and individuals function in our changing world, in order to transmit this knowledge to my students and readers.

Innovators have always interested me most. That is why I was particularly attracted by the concepts and methods of certain pioneers: Luciano Benetton, Anita Roddick, founder of The Body Shop, Edouard Leclerc, the controversial owner of a French supermarket chain and, last but certainly not least, Rich DeVos and Jay Van Andel, co-founders of Amway.

I must admit that when I first heard about Amway, ten years ago, I reacted like many people. I was skeptical, to say the least. It sounded just too good to be true . . . and legal. In fact, it was indeed legal! Today, however, I am the intrigued observer of a company whose universal human values have allowed it to cross any border and become a smash-hit private business with a cast of millions. Millions of employees? Not at all. The Amway network is made up of millions of independent, self-employed men and women throughout the world who now enjoy a quality of living often much higher than any ever dared to dream.

Who are these people? How did they succeed even though, most often, they had little or no business experience before becoming part of the Amway "family"? How does Amway help them achieve their goals without selling their souls? How do they become winners without having to compete in the ruthless world of ordinary commerce? How do Amway distributors develop not only their incomes but their personalities? How has Amway made the American dream come true for people in nearly 60 countries and territories? Who are the Amway managers and how have they succeeded in running a company based on people who own their own businesses? Why did these brilliant managers, who often previously worked for giant corporations, choose Amway, and why are they so devoted to its basic principle of offering opportunity to all?

The answers to these questions and many more are in this book, the result of two years of travel to 13 countries in North and South America, Europe and Asia where I interviewed top Amway managers and many local people whose lives have been transformed by their decision to become independent distributors for this remarkable company and its products.

But this book is more than a sincerely enthusiastic account of today's number one direct selling company. Impartial and uncensored, I have chosen to mention certain controversial issues which I invite readers to reflect on and judge for themselves.

Before wishing you a "bon voyage" through the world of Amway, I would like to thank its co-founders, Rich DeVos and Jay Van Andel. Thanks also go to Peter Scacco for allowing me full access to information and for respecting my right to publish all my findings.

Dominique Xardel

Acknowledgements

This book is the outcome of several years of close relationship with multilevel companies, and specially Amway Corporation. I am grateful to Peter Scacco, who accepted the idea of the book and facilitated most contacts with distributors and managers in different countries.

Among all the people I interviewed, I would like to thank specifically Steve Robbins, L. H. Choong, Takashi Kure, Ryunsuke Seto, E. H. Erik, Anita Ng, Eva Cheng, Low Han Kee, Alice Yeoh, Gladstone Pereira, Nortrini Bt Yacob, Anisah Bt A Razak, Richard Johnson, Jerry Rosenberg, Chris Bolsover, Stewart McArthur, Klaus Tremmel, Jim Payne, Jim Robins, Nicolas Lefranc, Greg Grochoski, Michael Rawlings, Bill Hemmer, Michael Anker, Roger Beutner, David Brenner, Trevor Lowe, Martine Heines, and of course Tom Eggleston.

Beyond this, the book would simply not have been possible without the help and criticism of Carol Bernstein and Susan Peter.

1

What Amway Is

The name Amway is synonymous with the American way of life. In 1959, its two "founding fathers" conceived their company along principles identical to those of the founding fathers of America. Sons of immigrant blue-collar workers, Rich DeVos and Jay Van Andel firmly believed that a land of opportunity is one where free enterprise prevails and where men and women of goodwill and independent spirit, by working hard and developing their potential, could better their lives and achieve the highest goals.

Were they just naive idealists, utopian dreamers? One might be tempted to think so, were it not that today there are over two million independent distributors who own and have freely developed their businesses. From all walks of life, a great many of these people did indeed start out with little more than goodwill and an independent spirit. They made a very small capital investment and often had no previous business experience whatsoever.

With sales of nearly US$ 4 billion (at estimated retail) in 1992, Amway is the leading business of its kind in the world and living proof of the immense possibilities of free enterprise. But just what is Amway and how does it work?

Amway makes over 400 household products and sells them, as well as thousands of other high quality brand name products. It sells them all in a way that allows people to shop without going shopping: through direct selling. This is a very general term for the marketing of consumer goods and services directly to people in their homes or the homes of friends or at their workplaces outside the retail store environment.

The direct selling industry grows each year and in 1992 represented a worldwide sales volume of US$ 45 billion. Often criticized, especially in Europe, because of the abusive practices of a tiny minority, at its best direct selling is based on trust, dependability, guaranteed satisfaction and warm human relationships.

Amway practices direct selling at its best. But it goes much further by combining direct selling with multi-level or network marketing (see box 1). In plain language, distributors do not just sell products to their friends, family and neighbors, they also recruit or sponsor people who become distributors themselves and in turn recruit others who become distributors who in turn . . .

Each distributor becomes personally involved with those he sponsors. He helps them to get started and to prosper and receives a bonus based on the sales made by his recruits and all the recruits they eventually sponsor. This person-to-person multi-level marketing process spreads from town to town, but also from country to country when, for example, American distributors sponsor relatives in foreign countries by correspondence or travel abroad to find new recruits and open new markets. Amway has been able to cross borders easily because it offers the universally-desired opportunity to lead a more comfortable, more independent and more meaningful life.

Box 1: Some definitions

Direct selling: The marketing of consumer goods and services directly to consumers in their homes or the homes of friends, at their workplace and similar places away from shops, through explanation or demonstration of the goods or services by a salesperson, for the consumer's use or consumption.

A sales policy based on interpersonal and human relationships, chosen by individuals and corporations, producers and/or distributors, who take the initiative of a direct and physical contact with consumers in order to offer goods or services at their homes, place of employment and, in general, outside the places generally reserved for sales operations which the consumers visit on their own free will.

Person-to-person direct selling:	Has been known in the past as door-to-door selling.
Multi-level marketing:	If a marketing plan compensates its participants not only for their own sales, but also for the sales of their recruits, and combines this override compensation structure with the distribution of products at various levels, that marketing plan is multi-level (or MLM as it is often abbreviated).
Network marketing:	It is used interchangeably with multi-level marketing. The difference is one of emphasis – multi-level would seem to emphasize the compensation method more, not just the distribution system.

Supported by Amway's state-of-the-art research, logistics, information and communications facilities, guided by the Amway philosophy of positive thinking, and motivated by the unique Amway system of ranks and rewards, distributors freely develop not only their own lucrative businesses, but their personalities and potential.

Amway's primary customers are its distributors who deal directly with their own customers and determine the retail price of the satisfaction-guaranteed products they sell. Free to launch a business with a small start-up cost, free to work at their own pace and to devote as much or as little time as they choose to their businesses, free to succeed not by competing with others but by cooperating with them, new distributors gain self-confidence and become more outgoing and sociable as their businesses progress. They are proud to have the power to open horizons for others. They find deep satisfaction and a great sense of security in being connected to a prestigious company that functions across the most far-flung borders like a closely-knit, supportive family. As Rich DeVos says, "Amway is more than just a company. It is a movement to help people help themselves."

Amway has "moved" fast . . . and very far. In fact, it now does more than 70 percent of its sales volume outside the United States!

By 1995, Amway sales in Europe are expected to surpass the American sales volume. Among other reasons, this is because a new spirit of free enterprise reigns there of which Amway is the very epitome. As Stewart McArthur, manager of Amway's strategy for Europe told me. "The most exciting Amway meeting I ever attended took place in Budapest in May 1992. There were 11,000 young Hungarians, from age 18 to 35, all new Amway distributors. They had tremendous energy and enthusiasm. They were absolutely committed to developing their own businesses."

American-born Amway is ranked number 8 of all foreign companies in Japan (source: *Weekly Diamond*). When I asked Jerry Rosenberg, who first came to Japan in 1972 as an English teacher and was in 1992 Marketing Manager of Amway Japan, the reasons for this success, his answer was a detailed analysis which revealed as much about Amway as about Japan. Here are just a few points he made.

Japan is a country where, by tradition, young people are supposed to be seen but not heard. They are not supposed to take the initiative, but simply obey and respect their elders. Married women are supposed to be discreet housekeepers who patiently wait for their overworked husbands to come home. It's no wonder then that the majority of Amway's Japanese distributors are married women or young single people. They all seized the Amway opportunity to assert themselves, to improve their self-image and to earn esteem, recognition, and added income!

The Japanese attach immense importance to their honor. They also demand that products be of very high quality. When a Japanese distributor takes an order from a trusting customer, he puts his honor at stake. The delivered product must keep his promise of quality. In Japan, distributors know they can trust Amway, just as their customers trust them.

Jay, Rich, Anita, Edouard, Luciano . . . and the others

I have called this first chapter "What Amway is." I would like to close it by showing that, in many important ways, Amway is similar to some of the other most successful and off-beat businesses in the world.

Each one was founded by an innovator who believed that priority should be given to people before profit. Each business developed spectacularly through original methods of management, marketing, networking or sponsoring.

Anita Roddick is the creator of The Body Shop which started as a tiny, very "marginal" cosmetic shop in the town of Brighton, England, and became a leading corporation. In her book *Body and Soul*, Anita says: "Business can be fun. It can be conducted with love and a powerful force for good. We have a basic understanding that to run this business you don't have to know anything. Skill is not the answer, neither is money. What you need is optimism, humanism, enthusiasm, intuition, curiosity, love, humour, magic and fun and that secret ingredient – euphoria (none of this appears in the curriculum of any business school)."

Frenchman Edouard Leclerc heads a network of nearly 500 giant supermarkets, each run by an independent entrepreneur who was sponsored by someone who was already part of the network. Edouard tells them all: "If you want to succeed in your business, you must consider your clients as friends and show them that you love them."

Everybody is familiar with the ubiquitous Benetton chain and its "United Colors", but very few people really know how co-founder Luciano Benetton functions. To quote one of his associates: "Luciano has a very special way of conducting business. He never gives an order. He only suggests ways of doing things. He is very reserved and discreet, shy even. He likes to work only with friends, with people in whom he has complete confidence. They all tend to act as he does. The whole network of 6,600 Benetton shops throughout the world was created and is still developing, through sponsoring:

friends, friends of friends, everyone has some relationship with Benetton agents or their relatives. It's all one
big family. Luciano's vision goes beyond business deals.
He and his firm are dedicated to what life is about, what
concerns everybody."

I do not think Rich and Jay have ever met Anita,
Edouard, or Luciano, but I am sure they would
understand each other perfectly because they share a
common language . . . and an uncommon vision of what
business is about.

2

What It Is Not

Over the years, Amway has often been taken for what it is not. I hope the following pages will help rectify certain false ideas and put the Amway image into better focus.

Amway is not a get-rich-quick scheme. Although it is true that thousands of Amway distributors have become more successful than they ever dreamed, not one of them did it overnight. Amway offers motivated, persevering people a precious opportunity. It does not serve them a prosperous business on a platter.

Amway is not just a "party plan", like Tupperware, for example. Party plan is a system of direct selling at meetings organized in the home of a host or hostess. Products are demonstrated, orders are taken, gifts are awarded based on sales volume and new hosts or hostesses are recruited. They sell products, of course, but do not always recruit in turn.

Amway is a person-to-person *multi-level marketing system* which allows each distributor to earn income from his or her own sales, the sales of his or her recruits, the sales of the people they in turn recruit, and so on all the way down the line.

As clearly stated by the US Federal Trade Commission in 1979, *Amway is not a pyramid structure* (also known as a Ponzi scheme after the dishonest fellow who invented it, or, in Japan, a rat scheme).

Pyramiding is an unscrupulous and illegal practice naive people often confuse with direct selling. In fact, illegal pyramid schemes are not "selling" at all – rather, they are direct fraud.

Unlike multi-level or network marketing organizations, pyramids generate income by paying money or compensation solely for the act of recruiting others. They are also characterized by significant "inventory loading" with little or no opportunity to sell the product.

Amway has often published warnings to people who might be misled into believing that certain companies function "like Amway", as their advertising fallaciously indicates. Amway (UK) Ltd, a member of the Direct Selling Association, recently published the following advice in a UK edition of *Amagram*.

Avoid any scheme which:

a   Encourages or permits any investment in goods for resale as a way of earning preferential discounts on purchases in advance of customer orders being attained OR as a way of gaining an immediate higher appointment in the organization.

b   Requires a participant to make regular fixed

payments in cash or by direct debit for merchandise or for any other service.

c Does not involve the opportunity for every participant to retail products to end users at a realistic profit.

d Involves a scheme whereby earnings are based primarily on the act of recruitment of others rather than a combination of rewards from retailing and from the retailing activities of others.

e Operates a fixed matrix structure which restricts the opportunity for recruitment by any participant to a defined number of people at any level.

Guidelines for spotting pyramid schemes

Over the past two decades pyramid schemes have been singled out for criticism and subsequently for eventual prohibition in jurisdictions around the world. However, pyramid schemes still persist in various guises.

The most dubious feature of such schemes is that income is generated from the act of recruitment of members rather than from the legitimate sales of goods to bona fide consumers.

It remains an unfortunate situation that many consumers associate pyramid schemes with direct selling and, therefore, any move against pyramid schemes could harm the image of the direct selling industry as a whole.

Towards consumer education, and thus, protection, a series of guidelines have been identified that can help the general public to avoid the pyramid-selling trap:

- Is the entry fee excessively high? Pyramid schemes insist on a high entry fee, because income is made primarily from the act of recruitment. In contrast, ethical direct selling companies charge only a modest start-up fee (generally less than US$100) and this is refundable.

- Is this fee refundable if a participant decides to quit? Pyramid schemes do not refund joining fees. Promoters of such schemes stand to lose money if participants ask for their money back.

- Is income earned from the act of recruitment rather than from the sale of the product? The main source of income that keeps pyramid schemes alive is the recruitment of new participants who need to pay a high entry fee. Income is based primarily on the act of recruitment. The very nature of pyramid schemes depends on an ever-increasing number of new participants.

Sometimes a product is used to disguise the emphasis on recruitment. For example, the purchase of a precious stone becomes a condition of membership. A stage is reached when new participants cannot be found. That is when the pyramid collapses.

Pyramid schemes seldom last more than two years, but at the end of that time, the promoters can have made a tidy profit at the expense of a number of members.

- Are the products in demand by the consumers? As the emphasis is on recruiting, products offered by pyramid schemes are generally of inferior quality with little or no prospect for sales to consumers.

Any product, if purchased, is retained by participants, and is not for sale to consumers.

- Can unsold products be returned for a refund? Most ethical direct selling companies offer a "cooling-off" period in case consumers change their minds. Also, ethical direct selling companies offer participants an opportunity to return unused, saleable merchandise back to the company for a refund (or "buy-back" policy). Pyramid schemes normally do not have a "cooling-off" period or buy-back policy. There is no refund of any sort to protect the interests of consumers and participants.

Members of the public are advised to exercise care when approached by companies professing to offer quick returns on their money.

There are basic differences that set legitimate direct selling companies apart from pyramid schemes (appendix 8).

3

The Direct Selling Revolution

Times are changing. Over and above political, technological and economic changes, new selling and marketing
methods are developing because of social conditions and
new life styles.

Today, a great many people yearn for, among other
things, independence, freedom to organize their working
hours, the possibility to relate to people whose company
they enjoy. They want to be rewarded as a function of
their time and the effort they invest in their activities.
These new mentalities have led to the direct selling
revolution.

One of the most important creative forces of this
revolution is networking or multi-level marketing. A
multi-level marketing business is one in which, "a
number of regular management functions, recruitment,
training, motivation and local distribution or products,
are franchised to independent distributors. It is a form of
mini-franchising where virtually anyone, with an
investment of the equivalent of $100 for a business kit,
can generate a second income from a part-time activity.

Direct selling is capitalism at its grass roots, and today there is a worldwide enthusiasm for small part-time businesses."

More than the development of privileged relationships between people of different horizons, networking is a state of mind . . . the state of mind of people who want to act freely, using their own methods and own pace. That is why networking is often called person to person marketing. The concept is far from new, but the different ways in which it is used prove to be astoundingly efficient and rewarding.

Of course, mass marketing is still alive. Even those companies, large and small, manufacturers and retailers, which used it exclusively are now reinventing their approach to selling, in business to business as well as for consumer goods. Roles are being redefined. A client becomes a salesman. But a salesman is also a client who can be involved in supply or manufacturing activities, and of course be paid for each role he or she plays. Telecommunications and computer technology make the intricacies of the networks manageable and controllable.

"What's in a name?"

Each one of the 12 countries of the European Community, plus Austria, Norway, Finland, and Sweden (a total of some 300 different business firms) has created a Direct Selling Association. Each national association is a member of the European Federation of DSA. In 1993, nearly 1.5 million people in Europe were officially involved in direct selling, producing the equivalent of 7 billion dollars of sales revenues.

There is a lot of confusion about terminology inside and outside the non-store retailing industry. The definition of direct selling given by the European Federation of Direct Selling Associations is as follows: "Direct selling is the marketing of consumer goods and services directly to consumers in their homes, the homes of friends, at their workplace or similar places away from shops, through explanation or demonstration by a salesperson, for the consumer's use or consumption."

Several countries use the term "in-home selling" or "in-home buying" instead of, or in addition to, direct selling. The direct selling industry does not use the terms "doorstep-selling" or "door-to-door selling" and considers them discriminating.

Direct selling is based on relationship marketing. If Management Information Systems (MIS) are important to deal with masses of data for business decisions, today Customer Information Systems (CIS) are also essential to appreciate the lifetime value of customers and establish lasting relationships with them. As a group of educators and practitioners emphasized, "relationship marketing relies on successful interactions between two individuals who enjoy what they are doing, even having fun, and who care about one another. The key to relationship marketing is culture, which starts with leaders, not merchants who view total control of a many-tiered hierarchy as the appropriate managerial style of retailing." (Direct selling Education Foundation, *A retail Agenda for the Year 2000*, DSA, Washington, 1991).

Moreover, today, a growing number of people seem to be willing to compete in a different manner. Instead of choosing to run in the same race, competitors choose their own race. As Edward de Bono reminds us, human beings tend to innovate, and in order to do so, have to use some methods to which they were not previously accustomed: "we must begin to develop systematic methods of serious creativity". This is exactly what, in the direct selling world, the multi-level approach is doing – concentrating on how to motivate people, to stimulate them to work and develop their own networks, so that they can sometimes make large amounts of sales through the diversified activities of the different networks they originate. As Peter Drucker, or Theodore Levitt have been repeating for 30 years, "the purpose of any business is to create and keep a customer." Direct selling, like any selling, is an activity where somebody starts by making friends with people who, in turn, generate names of prospects. As S. Rapp and T. Collins once mentioned, this is accomplished "through follow-up communications which build a bridge between the first impression and the sales, to the later interactions that keep you in touch with the customer after the first sale is made" – a continuum which turns likely prospects into long-term customers.

It is interesting to note the evolution in direct selling during recent years. Traditionally, since the beginning of the century, direct selling companies developed networks of *professional* salesmen, working full time for one company and relying on a formal hierarchy of field managers, district managers and regional managers. This is still the case for some firms such as World Book or Britannica, or to some degree for Mary Kay or Avon cosmetics in the United States and in Europe.

Then came the period of selling through *party plans*, the best examples of which are Tupperware, Stanhome or Nutri-Metrics. Party plans brought a new method of recruiting and identifying prospects through the organization of parties or meetings, most of the time in the home of the saleswoman or hostess.

Today, networking or multi-level marketing develops *a new way of organizing business* by stimulating a client to become a distributor and to recruit new clients who will, in turn, become distributors themselves. This new aspect of direct selling is being developed by a majority of the new companies which aspire to become members of the various Direct Selling Associations across the world. According to the President of the European Direct Selling Federation in Brussels, "80 percent of the companies who apply today for membership in one of the various Direct Selling Associations in Europe are putting into practice multi-level marketing."

It is no wonder that so many people are today attracted by direct selling, essentially because they can develop it as a *non-professional* activity, taking place in their leisure time. Often, direct selling becomes their favourite leisure activity, mainly because of the new people they meet and the new situations or problems they face, which are viewed as an opportunity to expand their knowledge of the world.

Within direct selling, the multi-level approach has its own rules, its own code of ethics. As an example, the DSA in America now stipulates that its company members must commit themselves to buying back at least at 90 percent of its cost any merchandise purchased but not sold by the distributors. Year after year, the multi-level industry is becoming more mature and is clarifying the rules.

The birth of a network

The first direct sales organization to develop network or multi-level marketing was Nutrilite in the United States in 1941. At this time, company salesmen received a bonus of three percent of the sales made by people they had personally recruited. As Peter Clothier reports, "when a team had sold $15,000 worth of goods, the head of this group was allowed to set up a 'breakaway' wholesaling relationship with the company, rather than his original sponsor. To encourage the formation of more breakaway groups, the company gave the original sponsor of the group an 'override' royalty on the sales of the new breakaway group. The whole system was rather primitive by today's standards, but it achieved the basic aim of rewarding distributors proportionately to the contribution they made to the overall profits of the company."

Rich DeVos and Jay Van Andel were distributors of Nutrilite when they created Amway in 1959, developing a different line of products and finally buying the Nutrilite company which today provides one of Amway's basic product lines. As a business concept, multi-level marketing has had a "long, slow, uphill journey" over the last 30 years in the USA, in Europe and in Asian countries. Today, several hundred companies practice multi-level marketing throughout the world. Most of them are members of the World

Federation of Direct Selling Associations which held its last world congress in Berlin in September 1993 with 700 participants from more than 75 countries. In fact, it represents more than 1000 companies worldwide, with some $45 billion worth of sales by over nine million distributors to some 320 million consumers.

In the United Kingdom, more than 20 firms today practice multi-level marketing involving over 320,000 people. In the United States, the number of direct selling companies is 110. In Japan, Amway started in 1980 and is now dealing with more than one million distributors in this country alone. In Hungary and Poland, which Amway entered in 1991 and 1992, after one month of activity in each of these countries, the company recruited some 40,000 distributors.

Direct selling is a business where a lot of people sell a little. The only difference is in the numbers of salespeople. Today, Europe has 1.5 million direct salespeople, the USA 4 million, and Japan has become the world's largest direct sales market with sales in 1992 of over $20 million.

Any distributor can have the possibility of developing business across borders. He or she first operates in one specific country and can later start sponsoring contacts in other countries by telephone, letter or personal visit. In this way, the distributor receives bonuses on international sales made by the groups of distributors he or she has developed abroad. Without living abroad, the distributor can also rely on the local company to assist his or her downline of distributors.

Happiness through self-sufficiency

As DSA explains, "retailing cultures are created that celebrate, even idolize, the sales organizations, sales associates, and customer service representatives – whoever is in direct contact with the customer. Motivation is created by a blend of compensation, special incentives, and recognition." In direct selling, sales forces are really independent, more self-confident, truly interested in work, and satisfied with their achievements. Learning – for both individuals and groups – is constant and seen as enjoyable. "A psychological principle is that happiness is a by-product of effort and achieved through self-sufficiency. Helping others achieve self-sufficiency creates the highest form of happiness." (See box 2.)

Direct selling organizations have learned how to recruit and develop leaders as well as managers. They are highly efficient in motivating people. They accept the need to empower front-line persons, focus on service and celebrate the sales force. They are incomparably aware that human beings have strong needs for self-esteem, and that this sense of accomplishment and self-sufficiency can be enhanced through motivation and recognition.

Box 2: Portrait of a successful distributor in 23 words

- Persistence
- Consistency
- Commitment
- Desire
- Exposure
- Goal-setting
- Solid foundations
- Positive attitude
- Self-image
- Enthusiasm
- Immediacy
- Big thinking
- Being yourself
- Professionalism
- Motivation
- Inspiration
- Association
- Education
- Delegation
- Communication
- Recognition
- Integrity
- Auto-suggestion

Source: Peter J. Clothier (1990) *Multi-level Marketing*
London: Kogan Page

4

One Plan for Everyone Everywhere

Amway makes over 400 products, but it is not primarily a manufacturing company. It is a marketing company. Its Sales and Marketing Plan, virtually unchanged for 35 years, was conceived to serve Amway distributors. An Amway distributor is an independent person who sells products made or selected by Amway. Whether you are American, Japanese, Mexican, Polish, British or whatever, you become an Amway distributor in the same way: once interested by the Sales and Marketing Plan, you agree to be sponsored by the distributor who explained it to you.

You can meet your future sponsor if you are already his or her customer for Amway products, of course, or if he or she is a friend or relative or business acquaintance. But you can also be invited to a meeting organized to explain the Amway Sales and Marketing Plan. Some successful distributors arrange these meetings regularly in their own towns. Others travel great distances cross-country to meet people and explain Amway to them. Still others go to foreign countries to find new recruits. Every Amway distributor in the world is free to recruit his or her own distributors anywhere in the world where Amway is authorized to do business.

If you are interested in the opportunity offered by a distributor, you simply fill out an application for a non-exclusive independent distributorship with no predetermined territory. It is valid for about one year but allows you to cease activity when you wish, no questions asked. Next, you receive the Amway Starter Kit.

The US kit contains essential information and full size products and costs about US$ 100. It is the only "investment" every new distributor must make. Other materials – book reviews and cassettes about positive thinking, self-motivation and suggested sales aids, for example – are available, but are optional. The one thing the new distributor must do, however, is to fully understand his or her two-fold mission as it is outlined in the Sales and Marketing Plan:

1   to sell Amway products to consumers;
2   to recruit new distributors.

The key to building a successful business is to create a good balance between selling and sponsoring. A distributor's progression, first to Direct Distributor and then to higher and higher ranks, and the added income and bonuses he or she consequently receives depend not only on his or her own sales but on the number of his or her recruits or "downline distributors" and their results. A distributor cannot however depend her recruits. An Amway distributor, by definition, sells Amway products. In order for him or her to receive a monthly Performance Bonus, based on the sales of his or her recruits, he or she must personally retail to customers and "turn over" 70 percent of his or her inventory every month.

The amount of this Performance Bonus is determined by two figures. One indicates the Point Value (PV) of products. The other indicates the Business Volume (BV), a dollar figure established for each product and totalled each month to determine product sales. Distributors earn Point Value and Business Volume by selling to customers, to other distributors, and also by using the products themselves.

I can well understand that many readers might be puzzled by the terminology and calculations of the Sales and Marketing Plan because it certainly perplexed me at first. New recruits also often have great difficulty understanding it. That's why it is their sponsor's responsibility to take the time to explain and simplify the plan for them and to give them all the support and advice they need until their businesses are launched. When you help new distributors help themselves, when you guide them instead of dominating them, when you cooperate with them instead of competing with them, you have earned their trust and their friendship. So it is no wonder that strong ties develop among Amway distributors of all ranks and that a fraternal spirit prevails.

Amway distributors are self-employed. They receive no orders from Amway management. They obtain products at approximately 20 to 25 percent discount and are perfectly free to sell them for whatever price they choose – or to use them themselves. But their freedom, like any freedom worthy of the name, presupposes that certain rules must be respected:

- A distributor must not take advantage of the association with other Amway distributors to advance any non-Amway business.

- A distributor must not sell or display Amway products or services in retail stores or other "public" commercial places.

- A distributor must accurately describe products (and their sales conditions) to his or her clients and must exert no abusive pressure to sell them.

A new recruit who devotes enough time and energy to his or her business can, within months, attain the higher ranks of Amway distributorship: Direct Distributor, Ruby, Pearl, Emerald, Diamond, Double Diamond, Triple Diamond, Executive Diamond, Crown and Crown Ambassador.

A Direct Distributor generates at least 7,500 BV per month for at least 6 months from his or her own sales and those of his or her recruits. Recognized as the leader of the group, the distributor may buy products, documentation and sales aids directly from Amway instead of from his or her sponsor. For each month that the distributor continues to qualify, he or she receives a "Performance Bonus" which is between 21 and 25 percent of his or her Business Volume. In 1992 there were tens of thousands of Direct Distributors in the world, most of them determined to attain a higher rank.

A Diamond Direct Distributor is a Direct Distributor who has sponsored at least six Direct Distributors. In addition to the Performance Bonus, a Diamond Direct Distributor earns a Diamond Bonus. In Japan alone, there were 124 Diamonds in 1992. The majority of them now work at their Amway businesses full-time, but they were originally trained as architects, musicians, teachers, designers, etc. They do international sponsoring in the United States where they have friends, and in new markets like Korea or Brazil which has the biggest Japanese expatriate population.

Double Diamonds are Direct Distributors who have sponsored at least 12 Direct Distributors and lead networks of hundreds of distributors. Trevor and Jackie Lowe, Double Diamonds, are the UK's top distributors. Trevor did research for a pharmaceutical company and Jackie ran a hairdressing salon when they started at Amway ten years ago. Their Amway business started slowly and had more than its share of ups and downs, but today, still in their early forties, they live with their teenage children in a beautiful 16th century house on 14 acres of land and are shopping for a yacht . . . and island property with a mooring.

Amway achievers also receive high cash bonuses.

But impressive as they are, financial rewards are not really what distinguish Amway from every other company in the world. As Rich DeVos says, "We have two forms of reward in the world. One is recognition and the other is dollars. We use them both."

Every distributor who has risen to Direct status has his or her name on a plaque in the halls of Amway World Headquarters.

Diamonds are invited to expense-paid seminars on the Amway yacht or in luxury hotels around the world to which they are flown on Amway planes.

High achievers are celebrated at rallies where they receive applause and recognition from thousands of members of the Amway family.

Hundreds of thousands of distributors have had their photographs printed in the *AMAGRAM*, Amway's full-color magazine with an annual worldwide circulation of 25 million copies.

"Motivating people, that's what I do best" says Rich DeVos. "Amway is a people business and so we studied their behavior. What are they looking for? What do they expect from others? Under what circumstances will they accept hard work? Once we understood these things, we built our marketing plan so it motivates our distributors and fulfills their hopes."

The Amway system of awards and rewards is not simple because the real motivations of people are not simple. As they change and grow, they constantly need to be encouraged, to be offered more and more. In over 30 years, Amway has used basically the same plan, making some improvements each year, adjusting it to the culture of each new country they enter, adding new awards, new bonuses, and new incentives of all kinds.

Why does Amway organize so many meetings and rallies, bringing together, at great expense, hundreds, sometimes thousands of distributors? Because people enjoy them. They like to be together, to cheer and shout and applaud those who have succeeded or soon will. They applaud as they like to be applauded when, sometimes for the first time in their lives, they go on stage and tell everyone about their positive experiences . . . and their failures. They discover that they can laugh at their own mistakes or weaknesses. They find new self-confidence in being able to say in public what they really think and feel. They know they will be listened to with compassion and lose their fear of being judged.

Why does Amway organize so many trips abroad for successful distributors? Simply to stimulate their imagination, to open their minds to other cultures and make them more aware of the diversity and richness of the world. Some distributors say that Amway is the best school they ever attended. In fact, the Amway business is becoming the world's largest university for people who did not have the chance to receive a higher education. And this might be its greatest motivational strength.

Amway's permanent staff produce a great deal of teaching and training material as well as programmes for building self-esteem. But there is another communication tool that is perhaps the most powerful of all. Every month of every year for over 30 years, Rich DeVos and Jay Van Andel have published a letter to their distributors on the first page of the *AMAGRAM* magazine. This page of advice, reflection, or just plain talk is person-to-person communication automatically transmitted to every single Amway distributor in the world. An example from the February 1992 UK edition of *AMAGRAM* is shown in box 3.

Motivating people, helping them to enjoy their work, is certainly the major challenge facing today's managers. Amway has understood this from the very beginning.

Just as it is impossible to describe the typical American, French, Brazilian or Japanese person without using senseless clichés, no description of the "typical" Amway distributor can have any value. There is just no Amway mold people fit into. Each distributor is his or her own person. Each couple (for Amway distributorships are often owned by couples) has its own way of functioning.

Box 3: "Reasons" vs Facts

Ever since we started Amway, we've heard a good many reasons why "it'll never last". After over 30 years, it's obvious that none of these "reasons" hold water, but we still hear them from time to time. Perhaps you and some of your people, especially new distributors, may be hearing a few of them, too. So here are some of the so-called "reasons" – and the FACTS.

"The products cost too much"
   Check the cost per use: that's what really counts. Every Amway product is covered by a money-back guarantee and always has been.

"You can't match the nationally advertised brands"
   We don't match their national advertising, but we do match or exceed their product quality. Plus you provide personalized service as well.

"Everybody's using Amway already, you've saturated the market"

Amway's market penetration, in most cases, is only a very small percentage. We've still a very long way to go before there's any danger of saturation.

"American lifestyles and outlooks won't transplant to other countries"

National governments differ, but we've found that people around the world welcome and appreciate the Amway opportunity.

"You've got to get in on the ground floor to succeed in this business"

Amway has no "ground floor". You have the same opportunity and chance of success today as distributors had over 30 years ago . . . .

"It'll never last"

Amway has more than lasted, it has expanded tremendously. But we believe the best is yet to come!

Richard M. DeVos
Co-founder and
Former President
Amway Corporation

Jay Van Andel
Co-founder and
Chairman of the Board
Amway Corporation

All over the world, however. Amway success stories often follow similar patterns:

- A young married woman with school-age children who has bought and appreciated Amway household products or cosmetics decides to use her free time to sell these products to her family and friends. Her business starts very slowly, but once it gains momentum, her husband, who was skeptical at first, devotes his weekends to helping her. Soon, sometimes very soon, their business becomes a lucrative part-time job or, in some cases, a full-time career. 80 percent of Amway businesses are owned by couples.

- A physically disabled person, looking for a way to become more autonomous, starts to invite people to his or her home to hear about Amway products and the Sales and Marketing Plan. One of Amway's Crown Direct Distributors is blind.

- A person with a good salary is dissatisfied because he feels no real pride in his work. He becomes an Amway distributor in his spare time, just out of curiosity. Within two or three years he has left his tedious job to become the responsible self-employed person he always wanted to be.

- A General Practitioner, a research technician, a social worker, for example, all love their work but cannot afford some of the comforts they yearn for. They become Amway distributors to supplement their income and improve their standard of living.

- A person living in an Eastern European country learns about Amway from relatives living where free enterprise is encouraged and rewarded. He dreams of being independent himself one day. Within one week after Amway opened offices in Poland, more than 40,000 applications were received.

- A woman of means is at first tempted by Amway not because of the financial opportunities, but because she needs the social approval and self-pride that come from working. Soon her business makes her feel she is a respected member of the community and her life is more meaningful.

- People living in poverty refuse to accept their situation and seize the Amway opportunity. One such example is the Bangkok noodle vendor who lived in a one-room chop-house with 20 members of his family. Soon after he became an Amway distributor, he was able to offer his family more comfortable living quarters and buy his first used car.

I could go on for many more pages describing the great variety of life situations which lead people the world over to take the Amway opportunity and use it to achieve their goals. But I think it would be more useful to remind readers that Amway is not a universal panacea. It works for people who can learn to think positively, for people who have an ideal, for people who are willing to learn and to share what they know with others. But it cannot help everybody every time. Here are a few of the reasons some people just cannot make Amway work for them.

All over the world, there are men and women who have been attracted to Amway's ideals and rewards and have taken advantage of the opportunity to be sponsored by a distributor. They have filled out the appropriate forms, received their Amway sales kit and made a first attempt to meet with neighbours or family members. So far so good. But when they were disappointed by their own "debut performance" and by its meager results, they immediately abandoned the whole project and chalked up one more failure on their long list of unsuccessful attempts to lead more rewarding lives. *Amway does not work for people who give up easily.*

Some people seem to be "born" distributors. They are sincerely enthusiastic about the Amway household or cosmetic products they use faithfully. They are sociable, hospitable and well liked. But as easy as Amway makes it for them, as supportive and helpful as their sponsors may be, these people remain obstinately incapable of correctly filling out a simple form, of keeping a clear record of any kind. Organizing meetings and sending out invitations are also part of the "paperwork" they claim is beyond them. Unless they have friends or grown children willing to do the part of the work they refuse even to attempt, sooner or later these "born" distributors will stop dead in the tracks of what might have been a thriving business. *Amway does not work for people who just can't get organized.*

Some people are extremely persevering and well organized but little else. In fact, they function more like machines than like warm human beings. They do not enjoy the meetings they organize so well . . . and it shows. Obsessed by the financial results they want to achieve, they see their guests and prospects as just so many stepping stones to success. If you do not buy, you do not rate with this type of misguided distributor who can look forward only to a very short career with Amway. *Amway does not work for people who do not like people.*

Strange as it may seem, there are many people who think they want to change their monotonous, predictable lifestyles, but are in fact unwilling or afraid to open their horizons. They may complain about receiving fixed salaries to perform routine tasks with no hope of advancement or excitement, but deep down, their foremost concern is job security . . . at any price, financial or moral. They are in a rut. Theirs, however, and one they do not care to get out of. People like this can be loyal Amway customers, but they are not motivated to become long-lasting Amway distributors. *Amway does not work for people who are afraid to get off the beaten path.*

Business considerations

Amway Corporation has succeeded for more than three decades in a highly regulated industry, because it is a proper, ethical, and honourable addition to the retail marketplace. Indeed, Amway is a worldwide leader in network marketing. A key element to this success is the recognition by federal and state authorities that Amway is a legal marketing system. In fact, the Amway plan is looked to as the model for others to follow.

As with any venture you consider, you should review all aspects, weigh the advantages, and decide whether it meets your needs. Some essential points to consider about the Amway business opportunity, and answers to the most commonly asked questions are shown in box 4.

Box 4: *Here are answers to the most commonly asked questions about the Amway business opportunity.*

Q. Do I have to sell products to retail customers?

A. Yes. Money is made in the Amway business through the sale of AMWAY products. Products sold to retail customers create the profitability of your Amway business. In order to receive a monthly Performance Bonus payment on the volume of your sponsored distributors, you must have ten retail customers during the month.

Q. How much money do I need to start?

A. About $100 for the Sales Kit. However, only the literature portion (about $35) is required. An assortment of AMWAY Products is *optional* (US only).

Q. Are there any hidden costs? Will I have to buy other business materials?

A. As your business begins to grow, you will want to buy products and you may wish to acquire training aids. You will also want to attend motivational and business-building meetings. But these decisions are up to you. There are NO requirements to purchase additional materials or services

---

Q. Will Amway make me rich?

A. Only you can make yourself rich. Amway is not a fast-buck, easy-money scheme. You'll find that your financial rewards will grow in proportion to the effort you put into your business.

Q. How much time will it take? How hard will I have to work?

A. Work as much or as little as you like. Typically, you may attend one distributor meeting a week. The rest is up to you. The bigger your financial goal, the more time and effort you'll have to put into your business.

Q. Do I have to sponsor people?

A. No, but many distributors want to and do sponsor other people. Why? Because sponsoring will increase your income when the distributors you sponsor begin to build their own businesses.

Q. Will having an Amway business save me money on my income taxes?

A. Your Amway business is NOT A TAX SHELTER, but you are entitled to deduct your normal and necessary business expenses as defined by your country's taxation laws.

Q. If Amway is such a great business opportunity, why aren't more people doing it?

A. Two million people around the world *are* doing it. And thousands of people, like yourself, are becoming Amway distributors every week.

© 1991, Amway Corporation, USA.

Start-Up Costs

Compare the start-up costs of this opportunity with that of a conventional business, and you'll notice quite a difference. The only cost is that of a sales kit for around $100.

Merchandising

The first way you can make money with your Amway business is to sell products to retail customers. Successful merchandising is made easier by Amway's broad line of high-quality products – a sound combination of upscale and consumable items that can mean profitable and repeat sales. Note, too, that product sales to at least ten customers are required to receive a Performance Bonus.

Sponsoring

You may increase your merchandising efforts through sponsoring. It's not necessary to sponsor people, but sponsoring may increase your income when the distributors you sponsor begin to build their own businesses.

Business Support Materials

As your business begins to grow, you may want to acquire training aids. You also may want to attend motivational and business-building meetings. These are optional, and the decision is up to you.

Deductions

Your Amway business is not a tax shelter, but you're entitled to deduct your ordinary and necessary business expenses as defined by your country's taxation laws.

Time and Effort

The bigger your financial goal, the more time and effort you'll need to put into your business. With an Amway business, you work as much or as little as you like, depending on your own goals. It's all up to you.

5

Exporting Opportunity

Amway believes all men and women can achieve their goals if they seize the opportunity to do so. Although there are innumerable personal goals that depend on the particular situation of each person, there is also, according to Amway, one practically universal goal: to improve one's standard of living and, by doing so, earn self-respect and the esteem of one's community.

The manufacturer of hundreds of products, Amway maintains that it is not primarily a manufacturing company. Its business is marketing. What it markets essentially is the opportunity to achieve the goal of self-improvement, which explains why the Amway concept, of American origin, crosses borders so easily.

But Amway does more than cross borders: it grows – and grows and grows – on all soils. Why? Because it is a perfect example of what is called a "trader's culture."

In international business, there are two opposing cultures: the trader's culture and the empire-builder's or conqueror's culture. An empire-builder's culture is a mechanistic or bureaucratic system, based on central government traditions. Although it must face an international marketplace that demands flexibility and speed, it is a heavy, slow-moving organization that inhibits individual creativity. Rigidly hierarchical and inner-oriented, it remains remote from local people, keeping them on the outside looking in.

Amway is a trader's culture. Based on trust and accessibility, people-oriented and "friendly", it is a self-renewing organization ready and able to face the challenge of rapid growth, changing work conditions and new cultures.

In his analysis of self-renewing organizations, Noel Tichy, a professor at the University of Michigan, Ann Arbor, Michigan, USA, remarks that they create "an environment in which people are highly interactive . . . people at all levels of the organization must be able to work quickly across boundaries, creating new teams and networks to solve problems and allocate resources . . . Boundaryless refers to the permeability of the functional, hierarchical, customer and supplier boundaries. While shared interests are the fuel that drives this engine, trust is the oil that keeps the parts moving without friction." (Lecture given in Paris in July 1992).

Amway is boundaryless too because by entering marketplaces the world over, it offers the same opportunities to people everywhere. As Rich DeVos expresses it: "Amway is a company that reaches down to where people live. When people hear of capitalism they think of a big company building a factory which may or may not give them an opportunity. But with Amway they don't just look at capitalism, they become capitalists." Instead of building a vast empire, of

41

factories, for example, Amway has created a federation of hundreds of thousands of private businesses, each well-rooted in its local community, but open to the world at large. Amway's strategy of identifying and promoting convivial business environments is a success because, to give just a few examples, American distributors keep in contact with family or friends in Canada and Mexico, Chinese people living abroad maintain family ties in Hong Kong and Taiwan. Mainland Japanese communicate with the vast Nippon community in Brazil . . . . The result is an independent worldwide sales force of two million people who now sell not only the products manufactured or commissioned by Amway, but also those made by other companies.

Today Amway gives its distributors even greater opportunities by including in their catalogs hundreds of new products including Coca Cola dispensers, MCI subscriptions, Motorola mobile telephones, certain Philips and Sharp electronic articles, travel packages, insurance, financial services, language learning systems and so on.

But if Amway can offer people all over the globe the opportunity to achieve their goals, it is also because Amway has seized opportunities to achieve its own. Here are just a few of the new situations which have opened the international marketplace:

- Asian economies have grown three times faster than those of the rest of the world. Some 72 million Asians – not counting the Japanese – have annual household incomes of $10,000 or more.

- Since the destruction of the Berlin Wall, nearly all Eastern European countries have been experimenting with capitalism and discovering the "tricks" of free trade.

- Today a non-European can fly to a European city, and then travel more freely than ever before to 11 other countries. And so it is with shipped goods, which now require a single document and can be transported from one European city to the next in record time.

National struggles for freedom and democracy, technological and social revolutions, demographic changes and economic booms have opened the global marketplace to corporations capable of meeting its challenges. Amway is one of them because it responds to a universal desire for self-improvement, but also because it has mobile, people-oriented managers and state-of-the-art communication and logistics systems.

Professional expatriates

There are about 30 of them. Every two years, sometimes every six months, in answer to the company's needs, each one travels from one country to another setting up new Amway headquarters, dealing with the particular challenges of each new situation. They know each other well, have from ten to twenty years of experience with Amway which, most often, was their first working experience. They see each other once or twice a year at meetings and are all well briefed on the problems each must solve. They communicate easily and regularly through satellites, electronic mail or computer networks. Some speak only one language, others are fluent in up to five languages. They all have the capacity to adapt quickly to new cultures, new friends, new living and working conditions. They maintain close relationships with distributors, accompanying large groups to faraway places for incentive seminars or attending local meetings in the evening or on weekends. Totally committed to Amway, from wherever they are, they keep in regular contact with World Headquarters in Ada, Michigan, by computers, telephone or fax. They are Amway's professional expatriates. Every one I have had the pleasure to meet really seems to love his or her work – work made possible because, again, Amway is a self-renewing organization where, writes Noel Tichy:

"Control is primarily self-control. There's less constraint; the emphasis is on learning with as few rules as possible. Errors are embraced. People admit mistakes, examine causes, and learn from them. There is an emphasis on risk taking and innovation: responsibility is realistically accepted and shared. Goals are set and constantly revised. Decision-making processes value intuition and creativity: there is less emphasis on purely analytical ap-proaches. People perceive power as a nonzero sum game: there is expansion in sharing. Uncertainty is confronted not denied. Interpersonal relationships are open and there are high levels of trust."

I would like to introduce some of these expatriates to you, describe their itineraries and also give you a small glimpse of how they solved problems typical of the countries to which they were assigned.

- Steve Robbins has served Amway in France, Guatemala, Panama, Brazil, and Argentina.

- Jim Payne managed Amway headquarters in Thailand before assuming the Director/Regional Manager's responsibility in Germany, Switzerland and Poland. Payne is now Director of New Market Development at Headquarters.

- Martine Heines had assignments in Belgium, Italy, Spain, France and the United Kingdom before becoming General Manager for Italy at Amway's Milan headquarters.

- Richard Johnson moved from Singapore to Germany and is now President and Representative Director of Amway Japan.

- Rob Davidson worked in Guatemala, Panama and Mexico before becoming General Manager of Amway operations in Korea.

- Chris Bolsover spent several years in Australia, then joined Amway Europe Headquarters in Great Britain, and later went to the US as Marketing Director.

To solve the day-to-day problems they were confronted with all over the globe, the professional expatriates had to be imaginative and capable of taking initiatives. Here are some examples:

- In Hong Kong where traffic jams are the norm, many Amway products are now delivered on motorbikes.

- Although it would have been more efficient to ship products to Korea directly from World Headquarters in Ada, Michigan, managers arranged to have a factory built in Korea to comply with government rules on foreign investment.

- To stand behind its distribution network in Brazil, plagued by runaway inflation and an unstable currency, Amway managers agreed to modify product prices daily, if necessary.

- In Thailand, where washing machines are rare, managers had the labels of its laundry detergent rewritten to provide instructions for handwashing.

- In Mexico and Pacific Rim countries where women tend to have darker skin, Amway conceived a new line of cosmetics in darker shades.

In fact, there are hundreds of examples of how Amway and its "people-first" philosophy supports and protects its distributors and their customers. However, it is not the philosophy that allows the work to be done. Often it is the superbly organized and efficient state-of-the-art structure of Amway World Headquarters in Ada, Michigan. To help the reader understand exactly how Amway functions with amazing efficiency throughout the world, the subject of later chapters, one must make a short side-trip back to "home-base" . . . the small American town where the Amway success story began 35 years ago.

6

Ada: The Heart of an International Network

More and more people already know the story of how Amway started in Ada, Michigan, 35 years ago. So I will just summarize it briefly before talking about what is happening in Ada today.

Amway started as a "basement business" – literally. In 1959, two men, friends since childhood, bought modest houses for their families in the village of Ada and used their basements as an office and warehouse for the products they intended to sell. Why did they start with household cleaning products? Rich DeVos' answer is simplicity itself: "We decided to sell soap because people buy soap."

But it was not just ordinary soap, because Rich DeVos and Jay Van Andel were not just ordinary entrepreneurs. They had the pioneer spirit and the very first product they made themselves was LOC, Liquid Organic Cleaner, one of America's first biodegradable cleaning agents. Why was this product so successful, even at a time when environmental consciousness was rare, and why is LOC Cleaner still one of Amway's best sellers?

Because it is a product of high quality. From the very start, devotion to quality has been an Amway principle: product quality, but also quality of research, of development, of manufacturing, of communication.

To start small and go on to great achievement, to start in a basement and to progress knowing that "the sky's the limit" is the American dream. Rich DeVos and Jay Van Andel believed in it and made it come true for themselves and for many others. Today Amway World Headquarters, still located in Ada, is like a city unto itself with three zip codes to handle over a million pieces of mail each month. Six planes, a helicopter and a team of 21 full-time pilots fly Amway staff and distributors to any destination in the world.

Research and development

On a mile-long stretch there are 81 buildings including the multi-million dollar *Research and Development Building* where hundreds of top scientists and technicians work in state-of-the-art laboratories: 12 devoted to product formulation, seven to evaluation, three to analytical research, one to toxicology and in-vitro research and another to electromechanical experiments. It also houses a staff of approximately 400 people whose mission is to unlock the potential behind every Amway product. The result is that 40 patents have been issued and 37 more are pending. A patent not only protects the uniqueness of Amway products, but adds prestige and credibility to the brand name.

49

On a recent visit to Ada, I interviewed Greg Grochoski, in charge of Research and Development.

Could you describe the steps leading to the development of a new product?

Greg Grochoski: Every new product begins as a concept. We get ideas from our Sales and Marketing Departments, from distributors and customers, and from our study of industry and market trends. After management approves the concept, we estimate the cost and prepare a development schedule.

Then, we designate a development team and team leader for the proposed product. The team develops a method to create the desired product characteristics – formulating and testing repeatedly until we reach, or even exceed, our original target.

Because we recognize that the package and delivery systems are just as important as the product formula, package development parallels formula development.

Following package testing – compatibility, stability, environmental, and toxicologal safety testing – we test the product with a panel of users. If we uncover problems at any stage – such as a product's smell, feel, or label instructions – we'll go back as often as necessary to produce a product that meets our standards of excellence.

Then we develop the product specifications for mass production in the plant. First, we do a test run. Then, if the prototypes meet all our criteria, we approve full production and market distribution. Even at this stage, we continue testing to ensure that the finished product is identical to the one we developed in the lab. At the same time, Quality Assurance, a department within the Research and Development Division, tests in depth to ensure that all production meets product designs.

How much time do you need to develop a new product?

Greg Grochoski: Anywhere from a few months to several years. It varies with the product. If it's an electromechanical product involving high technology or a nutrition product requiring long-term clinical studies in a medical facility, development could take three to five years. (If we're developing a new detergent and the materials are readily available, we still need sufficient time to develop good packaging to ensure the best performance and for panel testing, but the total time would be much less – anywhere from nine to 18 months).

The cost varies too – from several thousand (US) dollars into the millions, depending on the product.

How is Amway equipped to develop products for all the international markets?

Greg Grochoski: Fortunately, science is universal. Customs, language, and market needs and preferences vary from one market to another, but the science involved in developing and maintaining products is fundamentally the same. Here at Amway World Head-quarters, we've recruited top scientists in our industry who are fully qualified to develop the highest-quality

51

products for markets anywhere in the world.

Effective cooperation between our scientists and the marketers and distributors in the international markets is still absolutely essential. Our scientists obtain direction for projects from these sources.

Is networking used in research as it is in marketing?

Greg Grochoski: Absolutely. Networking is very important at Amway across the board. We have 42 laboratories here and around the globe . . . . We have development projects with many companies. We are using their labs, their personnel, their expertise. We have university labs that we fund research in, so networking is a very real term within what we do technically as well. We believe that good ideas come forward and we have open ears for them. Each week, I receive at least three ideas or product concepts. We take a look and see if we can make them directly, or if we have to change some features. One networking example is how we have matched up well to cultural changes in Japan, and as a consequence done well in that marketplace. Eastern Europe is in sociological change and we are striving to do the same kind of match-up to what is happening there. Being attentive to the marketplace, sociologically and culturally is the essential key. We constantly benchmark ourselves against what we think is the best in the field. Like networking, benchmarking is also becoming a key word in Amway.

Information systems

Ada is also the main artery of Amway's *Global Information Systems Network*.

From December 1991 to March 1992, a group of Amway executives from, among other places, Canada, Australia, Mexico, Europe and the Pacific Rim, met in Hong Kong, Tokyo, Munich and Ada to set up the strategic information systems plan that Amway will follow until 1995.

This plan will support the Sales and Marketing Plan by accepting a distributor's application, taking and fulfilling his order and paying his bonuses. It must also serve the management of every distributor's business by answering all questions about products, services, orders and group organization in order to leave distributors as free as possible for selling and sponsoring.

As David Braun, in charge of information services for Amway says: "Some aspects of Amway businesses are quite complex. Our objective is to simplify."

For a new distributor, to simplify means to give him or her an easy way to order and keep track of his or her activity. For those who have been in the business for a long time, to simplify may mean to give them a complicated computer program with so many capabilities that it will simplify the very large businesses they are running.

In Ada, where each month Amway receives about 200,000 calls from US distributors, the telephone systems are all computer driven. Computers will take orders by voice. If the distributor uses his or her own computer to send an order, the transaction will be made between the distributors' computer and Amway's computer.

Two hundred people work in the computer rooms of Ada, 35 in Munich, 35 in Tokyo. For Amway, information systems are a key factor of success since so much depends on the process of taking a distributor's order and delivering the product in good time, even though in some locations, you cannot always depend on telephone, roads, or mail.

In addition to data about ordering and delivery, daily inventory movement, finance, personnel and marketing, there are the procedures associated with the processing of data that must be specified by Ada. Around the globe, bonuses are always paid on the 15th of the month. The line of sponsorship is a complicated process and must be dealt with in a fixed procedural way, as must financial reporting. As Amway moves into worldwide networks, procedures for data transmission, encryption and compression are of key importance. The automation of all Amway businesses is a requirement, not an option.

Formerly at British Petroleum, David Braun is enthusiastic about Amway's possibilities. "Amway means new products, new markets, new services, new, new, new!! There is a willingness to change here, to evolve. New promotions for distributors, special bonuses, special incentives . . . to keep the distributor excited all the time we must get more efficient all the time. Every day 30 countries communicate information to Ada. A lot of it comes in the afternoon from Europe or in the process . . . ."

Manufacturing and purchasing

Ada is much more than the heart of Amway research. Most of the manufacturing of the company's products takes place there too, at a 3 million square foot plant. Some products are also made in Buena Vista, California, others in a factory in South Korea. A new plant is part of Amway's project for mainland China. All products are delivered to Amway distributors through over 100 regional distribution centers around the world, eight of which are in North America. In addition to its original household cleansers, Amway now manufactures over 400 products. "And we create new products every month, sometimes several a month," Roger Beutner told me. Senior Vice President-Operations, his responsibilities include manufacturing, purchasing, engineering and logistics. He calls Amway "A very exciting place because of the tremendous growth."

But Amway does more than create its own products; it also sells thousands of others through its PERSONAL SHOPPERS catalog. David Brenner, Senior Vice President-Marketing says: "We deal with hundreds of suppliers all over the world. We often have very long-term relationships because suppliers like to work with companies that are fair and faithful in their dealings." Situated in Ada, the Catalog Warehouse fills orders for more than 20,000 products, from appliances to apple-sauce . . .

Publications

World headquarters for research, manufacturing and information systems, Ada is also the site of Amway's immense printing plant. Every month, more than 1 million pounds of paper are used for scientific reports, for brochures about Amway's cultural and environmental activities, for teaching and training material, for PERSONAL SHOPPERS catalogs and for the North American editions of the *AMAGRAM*, the monthly magazine that is Amway's primary distributor recognition, information and motivation vehicle.

Published in 24 languages (Reader's Digest has "only" 17 different language editions), the *AMAGRAM* magazine is distributed every month on five continents to each and every Amway distributor. Although each country's edition features success stories of native high achievers and tells of particular merchandising offers, all editions the world over print the same monthly editorial, from Policy Board made up of family members and co-founders Rich DeVos and Jay Van Andel.

In the preceding pages, I have tried to show some of the many ways in which Ada functions as the heart of the Amway international network. But Ada is also, of course, the faithful and extremely efficient servant of distributors in America. Here are just two examples:

- The Telephone Ordering Department uses over 450 inbound toll-free lines and up to 450 full and part-time employees, depending on the season or holiday. It averages more than 14,000 calls per day, but can receive up to 30,000 calls in a single day. "Our goal is to answer 90 percent of all calls within 30 seconds of the time they arrive," says Roger Beutner.

- The Amway truck fleet logs more than 3 million miles a year (the equivalent of 100 trips around the world!) to serve North America.

In 1992, about 5,000 people worked in Ada. The total number of Amway employees, including overseas managers and their staffs was 10,500. For a US$4 billion business present in more than 50 countries and including over two million independent distributors and their tens of millions of customers, this is an amazingly small staff. But as Rich DeVos says: "The larger Amway grows, the easier our job becomes. We have a management team that really runs the company on a day-to-day basis and they deserve much of the credit for our smooth operation."

In other books about Amway, the starring role has always been held by distributors who have made remarkable achievements. That is why I have chosen to regularly give center stage to leading figures of the Amway staff, those "unsung heroes" without whom this remarkably co-ordinated network could not be what it is today.

7

Japan

There was very little applause when Amway entered the Japanese marketplace with just nine products. Many people in Japan had preconceived ideas about it. They thought Amway distributors used selling methods that exploited their family and friends. They thought it was a pyramid scheme like those recent legislation had banned.

Amway managers knew that the only way to overcome these prejudices was to communicate the Amway philosophy to Japanese leaders who would eventually make it understood. This did not happen overnight, but it happened. And today Amway Japan is the third most profitable US subsidiary in Japan and the fastest growing. Its value on the Tokyo Stock Market – where in 1991 Amway sold eight percent of its stock to the Japanese public – is estimated at $5 billion. In 1992, there were over a million Amway distributors in Japan, including over 4,000 Directs, 124 Diamonds, Double and Triple Diamonds and several Crown Ambassadors. Every month 40,000 new distributors are recruited. The renewal rate is the highest in the world.

To understand the reasons for this phenomenal success, while in Tokyo I interviewed the then Marketing Manager of Amway Japan. He maintained that certain realities of Japanese life helped Amway considerably.

- *Distribution is favored* by the Japanese infrastructure. Japan has excellent packing systems and inventory controls and also the most efficient small package delivery system in the world. Distribution is largely computerized and the educational level of the people is generally high, so it is easy to find qualified employees to run the distribution centers.

- *Products are adapted.* In fact, 25 percent of the Amway products sold in Japan are manufactured locally and so they really meet the needs of the Japanese. Quite a few new products, developed in Japan, are now being sold worldwide.

- *Distributors are motivated.* Mostly housewives and young single people, they enjoy social interaction and are often looking for different groups of friends. They also prefer to feel close to the company and value this relationship more than total independence. Since they want more control, the company implements more.

- *The philosophy is appealing.* Japanese like the Amway philosophy because it is American, but different from that of other direct selling companies. They appreciate the charisma of the co-founders and the idea that people can set their own goals. They particularly like Amway's public relations activities in favour of culture and the environment, a major issue for many Japanese.

He added that Japanese culture lends itself to sponsoring and that particularly close relationships develop between sponsors and recruits. A deep commitment is felt and Amway is trusted to come through with the promised services and high quality, of course, but also moral quality (see Amway Japan mission statement).

When someone becomes a distributor in Japan, it is rarely just for financial reasons. People are looking for self-esteem and the opportunity to do good work. They want their accomplishments to be recognized . . . and translated into figures. That is why Amway Japan has well publicized the fact that in 1991/92, the 106 Diamonds had an average revenue of 16 million yen, the 4,000 Directs an average of 4.5 million yen and the 260,000 active distributors 192,000 yen.

The Japanese enjoy being together, so in 1992 the company organized over 600 meetings and three rallies, each attended by 10,000 people in the Yokohama area. Amway also took 2,000 high achievers on a 4-day expense-paid trip to Hong Kong where they saw the sights and attended meetings.

Another interesting point concerned the structure of the Japanese language. It is very complex. Just to read a newspaper you must be able to recognize 4,000 characters . . . a far cry from the 26 letters of the Roman alphabet. This means that the complexities and subtleties of the Amway Sales and Marketing Plan do not discourage new recruits, who are accustomed to reading highly detailed documents.

In April 1992 I met Richard Johnson, President and Representative Director of Amway Japan. Our conversation took place in his office in Tokyo's ultra-modern Arco Tower. I asked him how Amway had changed since my first visit in 1983 and also about his own experience in direct selling.

Richard Johnson: If you construct a building without connecting rods in the framework, if you just stack things up, the ripple effect can destroy it. But if you put in the rods, you control the distortion and reduce the impact. It takes a bigger destructive force to harm it. Amway's integration with its distributors' lives, our distributors' philosophy, communications and behavior are the connecting rods that we must put in place.

Is this ripple effect specific to multi-level companies?

Richard Johnson: Yes. It is not specific to direct selling, but definitely to multi-level companies.

There are very few multi-level companies, I believe.

Richard Johnson: Avon is moving toward multi-level. Mary Kay should be considered multi-level. Pola in Japan is quasi multi-level. Most of the multi-levels coming in are looking for a quick pay-off. Amway's advantage is that Rich and Jay built a company that believes in the value of multi-level to the distributors and not just to the owners. That's why we grew so quickly.

But rapid growth means the connecting rods don't get well secured. When I was in Germany, business was booming and we were bringing in people who did not understand Amway.

What is the situation in Japan today?

Richard Johnson: Amway grew tremendously over the last three years, but for the last six months business has been flat. We have invested in our infrastructure and now have a senior staff of 20 people who are working on the connecting rods. We began to sense some bad ripples about 18 months ago. Instead of waiting until they expanded, we got rid of some people who were behaving badly. That eliminated the tremors but it also slowed down our rate of growth.

Do you consider yourself a part of the Japanese establishment?

Richard Johnson: No, and I'm not sure we would really want to be. It would be foolish if I surrounded myself with 65-year-old Japanese ex-Ministers to run our company. But, if we preserved our identity, we could eventually be part of the establishment.

Do you refer to Japanese lawyers?

Richard Johnson: No. There are very few lawyers in Japan. But we do work with opinion leaders and have excellent relations with MITI, the principal regulating agency. We will continue to build relationships across all the government ministries. Also, since my arrival, I have been very accessible to the press.

Do you offer specific services to Japanese distributors?

Richard Johnson: We employ 150 people in our telephone service open ten hours a day to answer distributors' questions. Every month we receive an average of 30,000 calls.

How does Amway compare with the other companies you worked with?

Richard Johnson: I worked with public companies like Procter and Gamble and Pepsi Cola which deliver projectible quarterly earnings. But trying to manage a direct selling structure from a quarterly earnings basis is doomed to failure. Here we have a volunteer army of one million people. When they wake up in the morning, they make a decision: Am I going to be a housewife or a salaried employee or an Amway distributor this morning? They make that choice again in the afternoon and once more in the evening. Our job is to encourage them to make the Amway choice. But we cannot influence them the way Proctor and Gamble can influence its sales organization. In this business there is a whole range of factors beyond our control. For example, when the school holiday season begins, we lose a lot of distributors because they go back to being full-time mothers. Our business is so volatile that it changes on a quarterly basis, although we should be able to plan on a three-year basis.

Will you make any profit this year?

Richard Johnson: We won't make as much as we would like. We will not match last year's performance partly because of some decisions we made in order to manage the ripples and partly to make sure we have an infrastructure to support the doubling of our business over the next five years.

What are some characteristics of Japanese distributors?

Richard Johnson: They are unusual creatures, independent, free-lance entrepreneurs. They have chosen to step out of the traditional role of salaried employees in order to run their own lives. You know, what brings me to the office every day is that the decisions we take here really change people's lives. The human factor at Amway is the most rewarding thing I have experienced in my working career. It is also the most frustrating, because people generally do not do what you want them to do.

The day-to-day relationship with distributors is the responsibility of Takashi Kure, Vice President and Chief Operating Officer of Amway Japan. He remembers the first three years when Amway was unsuccessful because leaders could not be recruited. As he says: "The company itself cannot be a leader, the development must come from the distributors themselves."

In 1993, the leaders are Crown Ambassadors, Amway's highest ranking distributors. Kaoru Nakajima, 41, was a musician and songwriter who worked for Yamaha. Shinzi Hamamoto, 35, used to sell records and

Amoto, his wife, taught music. Tatsuo Hayashi was a well-known drummer. E.H. Erik was a famous TV personality who introduced the Beatles in Japan. He and his wife Itoh Midori started as distributors in 1982. "We became Direct Distributors in three months and organized meetings almost every day. We became Crown Ambassadors in five years. Today I am 62 and I want to keep on going. If you want to motivate people, you must act as if you were a beginner yourself and continue to help other people grow and become themselves.

They will do the same for other people. This is what is most rewarding in this business: helping others grow and become independent . . . . Thanks to our activity, we have traveled extensively to Hong Kong, Singapore, Australia and most European countries. We also sponsor in Korea and have a group of 500 distributors in Hawaii . . . There is no secret about Amway: human beings and computers are the key factors of success."

Takashi Kure knows them all personally, of course, as well as the 124 distributors qualified as Diamonds. They are architects, musicians, teachers and designers, etc., most of them now working full-time in couples. They go abroad often to recruit, to the US, for example, where they have friends, or to new markets like Korea or Brazil which has the biggest Japanese population outside Japan. Japanese distributors who sponsored in Brazil get four percent commission on the business they generate there.

I had the pleasure of meeting Ryunsuke Seto, 36, who was a composer when he joined Amway in 1985. By 1992, he was a Triple Diamond with a group of 70,000 distributors in Japan. Most of our conversation was about the trees that he and his distributors plant to improve the environment. "At each meeting, our distributors contribute money to buy trees. Working for the environment is very important to us and we enjoy doing it. Last year, during the Gulf War, we gave money to clean the oil from the sea in the Middle East. We want to continue to be part of the Amway effort to preserve nature."

On April 23, 1992, I attended a memorable concert given by the 125 musicians of the San Francisco Orchestra, conducted by Herbert Blomstedt, at Suntory Hall in Tokyo. It was the first of 11 concerts in Japan and Taiwan entirely sponsored by Amway.

At the reception afterward, the Ambassador of the United States, speaking perfect Japanese, thanked the orchestra and Amway, and the President of the orchestra added: "A company who cares so much about the environment and the arts is an example for the world of business."

Box 5: Amway Japan Mission Statement

- The mission of Amway Japan is to contribute to the enrichment of our society and the prosperity of our company by providing a broad range of high quality products and services to the consumer.
- We will foster a quality environment for employees and distributors which stimulates high productivity, creativity, teamwork, trust and just reward.
- We will strive at all times to be conscious of our responsibility to society and to develop a sense of corporate good citizenship.
- We will conduct our affairs with personal and professional integrity, to assure continuity of the Amway business opportunity for future generations.

8

Europe

Until 1993, Stewart McArthur was in charge of Amway's strategy for Europe. He joined the company in 1977 as a Sales Manager, then, in 1986, began to organize the European market from Brussels. Today he has a staff of 30 people and headquarters in the UK. His job is to promote the company, enhance its image, keep close contact with all affiliates, rapidly set up management information systems and maintain a clear vision of the future. His objective: to build up Amway Europe as a single market while remaining flexible enough to adapt to the specific legislation and consumer behavior of each country.

Amway Europe was launched under difficult conditions. McArthur and his staff had to deal with complex problems stemming from administrative procedures different in each of the seven countries involved. There were inconsistencies in procedures, marketing approaches and relations with distributors. The French, British and German markets were particularly unruly. Between 1986 and 1989, Amway lost over $50 million in those three countries. In 1990–1, Germany and Spain caused tremendous difficulties because too much happened too fast. In Germany 240,000 new distributors were recruited in 18 months. As for the Spanish market, it grew by 1000 percent in record time, with sales that leaped from $10 million in 1990 to $120 million in 1992.

But this story, with its dramatic ups and downs, has had, to date, a very happy ending. From sales revenues of $70 million in 1989, Amway Europe moved to $105 million in 1990, to $265 million in 1991. In 1992, present in 11 countries, its sales were $350 million. By 1995, Amway Europe expects to include 15 countries with sales of $700 million. Its goal is to have one million distributors and service 20 million consumers by 1997 or 1998.

As Stewart McArthur explained, "After five years of experience, it is quite clear to us that we have to retain a high level of flexibility to make sure that we do not miss localized opportunities. In the German, Spanish or French markets, social needs are right for one market and not for another. About 70 percent of our efforts are consistent for all markets, but we must retain a marginal opportunity to do what is right by local market places.

"Amway has formed a very tight, low cost European center which has brought the strengths of each country together and at the same time greater levels of responsibility and accountability into all the affiliate operations."

When asked about the recent evolution of Amway Europe he replied, "One of the major changes in the last two years has been the blue-chip manufacturers who approach us. They see Amway as an organization with massive customer opportunities which would allow them to market their products in a totally different way. Clearly, we are eager to tie in to such opportunities.

"Anything we can do to increase our profile as a European exporter to Amway marketplaces around the world is of interest. We have become one of the largest exporters of perfumes out of France, mainly because of our sales in Japan and in the United States."

Would you also market financial services?

Stewart McArthur: I am very much against Amway getting involved in the direct selling of financial services which historically have a bad reputation with the consumers organizations in Europe. The last thing we need is to walk into another trap. We do sell services (discounts for hotels, subscriptions to TV channels). We had the opportunity to sell mortgages, pension plans, insurance, but I am against such initiatives at this stage in our development. I think it is too dangerous.

Direct selling throughout the world is never viewed with total credibility. I do believe Amway in Europe has a better image and greater credibility than in other parts of the world. But knowing our problems, seeing the organic rules we already have, I think there are other and safer opportunities than selling financial products at this moment.

We should be focusing our resources in the area of health and beauty. We have products of outstanding quality whose price–margin ratio is far less important than some of our more basic commodity products. We are involved in a product sector which is exciting, faddish and consumer friendly. We can market our products in a sector where customers like to buy the very best and we have far more to do in that area of introducing products in existing markets and expanding the product range. We have a massive opportunity there without spending a lot of money in the areas of new products.

Our challenge is to find and to place differentials which allow all people in the selling chain to make some money. These two issues are clear in our market efforts. There is far more that we can still do in selling Amway-brand products. Our research indicates that two out of three Amway customers who bought in the past would buy again. To market more Amway products through our network, we should let brightly visible, well-known manufacturers raise our image and credibility.

Will you develop catalogs?

Stewart McArthur: Three years ago we launched the European catalog. This is the only catalog in Europe which sells the same merchandise across ten countries in six languages. It has been a significant added-value to our business – $70 million in 1992. This catalog has raised much excitement in our network.

In benchmarking, how do you compare with other companies?

Stewart McArthur: The company has been very tardy in trying to benchmark its performance in terms of service and commitment to the community. We have been too busy doing other things. But in the next few years we will have to ask ourselves who we are, who we want to be, who we want to be compared with and also how we are operating within our own standards. Until now, we have not always enforced our own rules when some distributors behaved abusively. We must be able to act before the level of commercial volume and profit becomes so attractive that taking action becomes very difficult. In Spain, for instance, we are dealing with a business which grew from $10 million to $200 million in two years. The number of sales creates a visibility issue, a credibility issue. We may have been too tolerant in the past with distributors who do not respect our rules.

How do you face the economic crisis?

Stewart McArthur: What is crisis? The quality of life in the UK is significantly higher than it was ten years ago. Crisis becomes relative. Without any arrogance, and based on our history to date, Amway seems to thrive in times of price recession. In difficult times, people look for other sources of revenue to supplement their existing income. We might be recession proof! We may even profit from recession. I try to see the future by focusing on the population of each country. Eastern European countries may develop very fast but other, older markets will still grow because of their population. For example, the United Kingdom is today an extremely successful market. It came back very strongly in 1991 and 1992.

The United Kingdom

Amway UK was one of the first international affiliates. Established in 1973 at Milton Keynes, near London, in 1993, it had over 40,000 distributors. The UK operation has grown into a major force in personal selling and operates from a complex servicing the United Kingdom, Jersey, Guernsey and the Republic of Ireland. This "high tech" facility is designed to provide all the necessary support in administration and delivery systems.

Amway is justly proud of its speedy order fulfillment: the warehouse is fully computerized and automated to provide continuous support to the distributor network. Orders are processed quickly and products are delivered efficiently and without delay. For the distributors' convenience, there are also two Product Selection Centers (PSC), at Milton Keynes and Crayford, Kent.

When asked about the situation of Amway UK early 1993, Stewart McArthur said: "It is an unusual situation. This is the only country in Europe with a pyramid legislation in place and Amway UK is called a legal pyramid! We are lumped in with multi-level companies of that kind. So, in 1992, we organized a programme of communication where we brought together thousands of distributors and had them all send letters of concern to their Members of Parliament, restating Amway's credentials. The objectives of the campaign – the Amway Business Awareness Campaign – were to promote the concept of multi-level marketing (and thereby to counter the association with pyramid schemes) and to persuade the Government to change the existing Act and Regulations to give the general public more confidence in this method of trading. After all, there are some very legitimate and ethical multi-level companies and they should be allowed to do business.

Thanks to our Awareness Campaign, each Member of Parliament received an average of 40 letters. At a House session, 340 members publicly stated their support of Amway. We also received very good press coverage. So we've decided to do the same thing in Spain, in Germany and in France because we want to get the message across that we are Amway and proud of it. We want to promote Amway as a symbol of free enterprise."

Eastern Europe

Do you expect big developments in Eastern Europe?

Stewart McArthur: In Eastern Europe we have brought countries the ideal they were looking for: a low cost independent business opportunity where the only thing you can lose is your time. With $100 you can start your own business and have the opportunity to get involved with hundreds of other people. Our attraction has obviously been powerful in East Germany and in Hungary. In Poland, in the first month we had over 40,000 distributors. It is a massive logistics challenge, because we are developing a staff with no or very little Western experience. But we were very successful in Hungary and in Poland.

Early September 1992, at Warsaw University, Amway co-sponsored a three-day seminar on small business for 700 Polish citizens who replied to an advertisement in a Warsaw newspaper. In all, 1,500 people replied. Several well-known Polish experts agreed to lecture free of charge as a public service. Among them were Andrzej Wroblewski, Editor in Chief of Gazeta Bankowa, Joan Edwards, Commercial Attaché of the US Embassy, Andrzej Sadowski, Director of the Adam Smith Foundation, Thaddens Kontek, Director of the US Peace Corps and small business Group, Jerzy Osypowicz, Vice President of the American Chamber of Commerce, Gertruda Swiderska, Price Waterhouse, Gabriel Wujek, a lawyer, and Henryzka Bochniac from the Ministry of Commerce. Also present were executives from Coca-Cola and Burger King the other co-sponsors. The team of lecturers was coordinated by Sławek Gorecki in Warsaw and by Michael Rawlings of Amway European Corporate Affairs in Brussels, a former laywer assigned to image-building.

For three days, in the Warsaw University auditorium, the largest academic space available in Poland, courses were given on capitalism, entrepreneurship, business ethics, investment and banking, wholesaling, retailing, franchising, and direct selling. All the lectures were video-taped and shown later on Polish Regional Television.

Responsible for new markets, Jim DeVos, after 18 years at Amway, had his first international experience in Mexico. Later he was sent to Hungary to prepare for the company's launch. "Usually it takes us between 24 and 36 months to investigate before we enter a market. Once we are sure of the opening date, we inform the distributors four months in advance. Before entering a market, we must be able to answer two questions. Can we go in and stay in that market? Is a wholly-owned subsidiary possible?"

He described how Amway sponsored a performance of the Chicago Symphony Orchestra conducted by Sir Georg Solti. Solti, a Hungarian, had been conducting the orchestra for 22 years, but he had never had the opportunity to perform in his homeland. Amway gave him that chance on November 19, 1990. The "homecoming concert" in Budapest was a marvelous, very moving event. It made Amway known for the first time in Hungary, where it was planning to open in June 1991.

In the first month after the launch, 35,000 people filled out applications for distributorship. In the second month, 45,000 people applied. Ninety percent of them were sponsored internationally by some 1,700 distributors who came from Germany and Austria as well as the United States, Canada and Australia.

The biggest challenge was handling this "overnight" success in a country with no communication infrastructure and no banking system. Today Amway sells 25 products to some 60,000 distributors who must collect them from one of eight distribution centers where payment is made in cash. Amway's turnover in Hungary is about the same as in Austria where there are only 18,000 distributors.

Jim DeVoss explained that because of incidents – in Austria and Czech and Slovak Republics, for example – where distributors started selling before products were locally available, no more new markets are opened until

Amway can properly support them with a central warehouse. Distributors who really want to reach the highest goals can now do so because there is product availability and also a simplified product range. This was decided in order to make things as easy as possible for people who, because of their political and social situation for the preceding 45 years, had so many things to learn. The concepts of direct selling and multi-level marketing, the most basic techniques of building, owning and operating a business, are sometimes assimilated slowly by people for whom free enterprise was not taken for granted as a fundamental right.

Germany

Amway Germany is run from its Puchheim headquarters by an American, Jim Payne, Director/Regional Manager, assisted by an Australian, Michael Anker (Sales Manager), who has now taken over the management of the German and Swiss affiliates. They have a staff of 300 people to deal with about 150,000 distributors, 120,000 of whom operate in former East Germany.

Jim Payne has worked for 12 years with Amway, first in domestic sales and then in international activities. From 1987–90 he was General Manager of Amway Thailand. He was transferred to Germany in September 1991. "The growth we experienced in Germany was absolutely phenomenal – 800 percent in one year! But now it has stabilized."

Did the boom really take you by surprise?

Jim Payne: Nobody anticipated the phenomenon. For 40 years, the East Germans had been shut out of free enterprise. They could have no concept of it, no understanding. But after the fall of the Wall, business exploded overnight . . . and created a great number of problems for us. There was no way to get the products to the distributors because of the lack of infrastructure. We had to set up stores – Product Service Centers – throughout the East. Distributors would walk in, pick up products, pay cash and walk out. There were no banking systems, and not enough phone lines. In six months we opened seven PSCs, but we had difficulty finding adequate facilities. Nothing was available.

How would you describe the German market?

Jim Payne: It's a market with a lot of ups and downs. Once West Germany had 80,000 distributors, but today it has only 30,000. Business is picking up because of the destruction of the Wall and because a lot of distributors have learned from the mistakes they made in the early 1980s. You know, when the Wall fell, there was no announcement that Amway would operate in the East. People just went there and a market, driven by sponsorship from the West, came into existence practically overnight. Amway had a small center in Berlin and people would drive for three or four hours to pick up their products. The East Germans didn't know what service meant. In one year, we spent well over 10 million Deutsch Marks teaching people about Amway. Today, people in the West are earning money from people in the East and vice versa. They are supporting each other in an interesting melting pot.

Sponsoring was an entirely new concept for the East Germans, but they caught on quickly. Today they recruit mainly in the East, but in the future they will come to the West because of the high population and better long-term potential. They'll come to the West when they gain greater confidence in their business abilities. It is a kind of wave effect. And the wave will start coming back.

Amway made the East Germans realize that, like everybody in the world, they too enjoy recognition. In 18 months 14 distributors became Diamond, one became Double Diamond and three became Executive Diamond. No other Amway affiliate had ever experienced that kind of growth.

Have you had problems with German legislation?

Jim Payne: Germany is a very legalistic state. There are restrictions not only about direct selling but about commerce in general. Stores, for instance, are open only during certain hours. There are strict environmental laws, too.

Michael Anker is Germany's newly appointed General Manager. After several years in the Sydney office, Anker learned German and now maintains close relationships with distributors. "Here," he says, "the business is the same as in Australia. The market is ten years old but in fact it is a brand new business because of the reunification. Distributors around the world are very similar: they want to change their life-style, they are hard working, very easy to deal with. They have set a goal and they want to achieve it. Some people want to send their children to a better school. Some people want to build a house. Some people want a faster car. Some people want all of it and a lot more. Some want to make a little more money, some want to make a great deal of money."

In Germany three distributors are responsible for 99 percent of the business. Mueller-Meerkatz and Schwarz have been with the company for 20 years, and Backhaus for nine years. All would be significant leaders in any business they started because they are very hard workers: six days a week and meetings and rallies almost every night, with a lot of international travel. They are incredibly dedicated in working down the lines they have created and they do it the way they enjoy.

Many German distributors have also developed a business in Austria, in Hungary and in Italy by international sponsorship. As Michael Anker underlines: "There are all kinds of persons, from a farmer, a professor, a civil servant to non-professional (part-time) or totally professional person. To succeed, you do not need a university degree, or to be a professional salesperson! And beyond their activity, I am amazed by the number of them interested in charities – particularly concerning children. A great many are dedicated to environmental protection. Yes, I am excited, not only about what happened here in the past two years, but about what will happen in the next ten years. It will be a huge business!"

Austria

Klaus Tremmel manages Amway Austria from head-quarters in Vienna. He is also responsible for Amway activities in Hungary where he spends at least two days a week as a rule. He has built up a solid business in Austria and maintains close contact with his key distributors. "Austria is very cosmopolitan. It is a mixture of everything. Different regions have different laws, so if you want to plan for the future, you must understand the history of the country," he says.

Tremmel has 53 people on his Austrian staff and 50 in Hungary. I asked him to explain the development of Amway in the two countries.

"As you know, Amway is not a normal business. It is a family business for the most part and the company itself plays the role of the family. Our biggest asset is that we are not organized. We are very flexible, constantly ready to change. People take on responsibility because they understand that it is necessary. They help each other. Essentially, that is how we grow."

I agreed that in today's changing world, the best management appears to be loosely organized or not organized at all. It encourages initiative and appreciates imagination: two excellent ways to motivate people. But, in reality, to succeed in functioning in this way, the company must be rigorously organized, have solid information systems and adhere to its rules while taking into consideration the sensibilities of the people who are loyal to it.

Klaus Tremmel explained that developing European coherence is not an easy matter because of the variety of cultural particularities. Since most Direct Distributors travel very often, they must be well informed about what is happening in other countries. They would, of course, prefer procedures between countries to be consistent. He gave the example of Max and Marianne Schwarz who are Crown Ambassadors in Germany and sponsor in Austria, Italy and Hungary. They are, in fact, Amway's biggest distributors in all these countries. But every month the Schwarzes receive their commissions and bonuses in German Deutsch Marks, Austrian Schillings and Italian Lire. However, Amway's globalization effort will soon permit them to receive a consolidated sum each month in the country of their choice.

Italy

Amway's Italian market now has nearly 30,000 distributors. It is managed by Martine Heines, a Frenchwoman who joined Amway in Ada in 1976 after working as an interpreter in Grand Rapids. She speaks five languages and was directly involved in preparing the French market and then the Spanish and Italian markets. She has seen the marketing plan evolve over the years and new incentives added regularly. She also participated in the often very difficult discussions with distributors who were unfaithful to Amway's ethics and philosophy.

"With so many distributors in a single country or operating in different countries, inevitably some do not play by the rules. Amway has always spent a lot of energy in keeping the network clean. Our credibility depends on it, especially since we promote the free enterprise concept and treat each distributor as an entrepreneur, free to work at his own pace and in his own way. He must, however, keep to the rules of his contract with Amway."

The Italian market grew slowly, but from 1991 to 1992, sales increased by 100 percent. To deal with this sudden growth, Martine Heines and her Communications Manager Monica Milone must maintain a delicate balance between their rigorous management and the liberal attitudes of their ebullient distributors.

Spain

Amway de España opened in 1986. It grew slowly at first because the important direct selling sector in Spain must deal with a very grey area in regulations concerning their legal and fiscal status. In its third and fourth year, however, business began to make important strides. By 1990, Amway de Esapaña had gained so much momentum that distribution, order processing and data systems could no longer cope. Sales in 1990–1 grew by more than 1000 percent and by 1992, sales had exceeded US $100 million and there were some 80,000 active distributors.

Such growth was clearly difficult to sustain. Stewart McArthur, Managing Director of Amway Europe, agreed that the company was hard-pressed to keep pace with such explosive growth scenarios. "As a company, we must ensure that our internal systems match the anticipated growth of our business. That is simply good strategic planning. But with the kind of growth we have experienced in the past two years in Spain, that is very difficult indeed. While we, of course, are delighted to see that the Amway concept has succeeded so well among Spaniards, the key now is to ensure that there is a proper balance between the dynamism of the growth of our distributor organization, and our corporate ability to absorb that growth and to constructively channel the dynamism."

In fact, Amway de España has responded internally to the dynamic growth in a number of ways. "The most visible manifestation was our establishment in 1992 of a new headquarters facility in Barcelona," said Stewart McArthur. "More clearly than words can, it reaffirms Amway's will to continue long-term in the Spanish market by enabling us to do a first-class job of improving services for our customers and distributors and to provide a first-class work environment for our more than 200 Spanish employees."

The new facilities in Barcelona's Zona Franca include 2,000 square meters of modern office space, 65 telephone lines, 4,000 square meters of annex warehouse space, and a state-of-the-art IBM computer system, which alone represented an investment of more than one million dollars. "We now can say with confidence," said McArthur, "that we really are totally capable of handling in the most efficient manner the 2,500 daily orders being generated by our dynamic Spanish business."

Such growth engenders external challenges. Peter Scacco, Director, International Public Relations, explains:

"Many of the external challenges strike at the credibility of the Amway business concept. Meteoric growth creates a high level of public visibility, attracting the attention of our competitors, consumer organizations, regulatory agencies, and, of course, the press."

Scacco, who has served Amway in Paris, Tokyo, and Brussels, has witnessed these reactions before. "Among other things, it is a matter of how we are perceived. Amway is a phenomenon which generates enthusiasm and energy, often expressed in ways which don't seem to mesh with the local culture. Indeed Amway brings its own unique culture with it."

It is difficult, but essential, to develop programs of public communications and education. Scacco says: "There are multiple communications issues which must be dealt with. The press, for example, needs to be educated about Amway's long and successful history as a company which manufactures a very broad range of quality products. It must also be understood that Amway's success has been global and has not happened overnight."

One criticism which has surfaced in Spain is that Amway is a pyramid scheme. "The fact is," argues Scacco, "that the Amway business concept has been tested time and again the world over. We've had agencies such as the Federal Trade Commission in the United States spend years investigating us and they concluded categorically not only that Amway is not a pyramid, but that Amway, in fact, brings a welcome alternative distribution channel to the marketplace. We've had similar discussions with officials in Japan, in Taiwan, and in the UK. We do not shrink from such scrutiny, because the Amway business concept is rock solid.

"Of course, it takes time for some people's suspicions to be surmounted, for them to understand that there is nothing inherently deceptive about Amway, that it is not some kind of sect, that it indeed is a unique opportunity for individuals to develop as small business entrepreneurs in an age when that is becoming increasingly difficult."

In Spain, Amway has been gradually building up that understanding with consumer groups, the press and the public in various ways. "We've taken journalists to the US to show them our enormous manufacturing operations, our commitment to quality through major R&D and QA facilities. We have had them meet with our top management. The net result is that they start to think that Amway indeed is a serious business."

Amway de España has also maintained an active program of product publicity, run a series of advertorials in major Spanish dailies and magazines, and hosted a number of meetings with Spanish consumer organizations. "One of the unmistakable messages," says Scacco, "is that a company which makes as large an investment in facilities, products, and people as Amway does, and which has delivered quality products to millions of loyal consumers around the world for many, many years, must be doing something right! It cannot possibly be an illegal pyramid. It must be treated seriously. We already are seeing some results in the press, which is now showing a certain respect for Amway as a serious company."

Communications must also be developed internally. "We have made concerted efforts to step up our distributor education and training programs in Spain," noted Stewart McArthur. "It is not enough merely to have first-class technical support systems – we must ensure that our distributors operate their businesses correctly. Company efforts are important, but the image of Amway is formed to a great degree by the behavior of our distributors every day out in the field with customers, prospects, and at meetings."

9

South Pacific

By the year 2000, Asia is expected to have two-thirds of the world's population and a gross national product higher than those of North America and Europe combined. But Amway did not wait until Asia was sure to be a booming marketplace. It opened its first Asian headquarters in 1974, in Hong Kong.

Hong Kong

Developing direct selling in Hong Kong was a formidable challenge. Amway's slogan "Shop without going shopping" did not sound very attractive in a place considered to be a shoppers' paradise. Because of the density of the population (six million) and the exceptional variety of goods available, shopping is convenient, highly organized and seems to be Hong Kong's "raison d'être". Bob King, former President of the US Direct Selling Association in Washington, DC used to say: "If you can make direct selling work in Hong Kong, you can make it work anywhere else in the world."

Amway made it work, but progress was very slow and the road to success was very rocky. In fact, it took Amway ten years to show profit in Hong Kong and to have its first Direct Distributors!

The sales curve leveled and consolidated in 1984, then made a big leap in 1985–6. And then the trouble started . . . and lasted for two full years. The largest Diamond group of distributors was discovered to be selling products from competing companies such as Shaklee and Avon through the Amway network, in complete disobedience of Amway Rules of Conduct, which state that "a distributor shall not produce or procure from any source other than Amway any item upon which the Amway name or logo or any of its trade names for trademarks is imprinted." They also betrayed the rule prohibiting distributors from attracting customers through various channels of promotion such as letter box drops or mass mailings.

How did Amway react? In 1987, after sending several warnings, it terminated a Diamond Direct Distributorship and thirty Direct Distributorships. As Eva Cheng, Managing Director of Amway Hong Kong remarks, "It was a very challenging period. I made the decision with full support from headquarters. The company is entirely committed to its distributors, but commitment must be mutual. It was a tough decision because we did not know how long we would need to recuperate. The business dropped by ten percent but the decision created a greater bond, unity and commitment to the company."

In spite of its very slow start and all the difficulties, Amway Hong Kong had very strong growth between

1988 and 1992 with 30,000 active distributors and 100,000 on file who each month receive the *AMAGRAM* magazine, published in Chinese and English. Among the 25 Diamond Direct Distributors, Anita Ng became Crown Ambassador in August 1991. I discussed her career with her one day on the 26th floor of Citicorp Centre where Amway Hong Kong has its head office.

When did you become a distributor?

Anita Ng: I joined Amway in 1981 when I was a Customer Services Officer at a courier company. I was 22 years old. I became a Direct Distributor in January 1983.

How long did you need to qualify as Diamond?

Anita Ng: A little more than two years. It took me another six years to become Crown Ambassador.

You must have worked very hard . . .

Anita Ng: I accomplish a certain amount of work every day. I keep a steady, very ordinary routine. I never work particularly hard one day and let myself be idle the next. In fact, my working day is no longer than an average worker's.

Now, you have reached the peak, you could rest . . .

Anita Ng: Certainly not. I like meeting and interacting with people, so Amway is exactly the sort of work that I really enjoy. I love to see others starting from scratch like I did, and attaining all the rewards that I once achieved.

You get a lot of satisfaction in helping people succeed. Amway is a long-term business. It does not offer quick money. If you want quick money, you are not suited for this business.

What do you plan for the future?

Anita Ng: My goal now is to have 20 Diamonds in my group by 1993. I am also prepared to move to China and other markets, when they open, because I believe that the potential of those markets is just immense.

You will travel extensively?

Anita Ng: I already travel with distributors for seminars and meetings. I am also invited to speak at rallies. I went to Japan, Canada, Thailand and recently to Taiwan where I spoke twice at conventions of 10,000 people each time. Amway gives us the opportunity to develop friendships internationally and I can share my experience all over the world.

Eva Cheng is responsible for Amway Hong Kong, for Taiwan operations and for the preparation of the new Amway market in mainland China. She graduated from Hong Kong University in 1975, worked for two years for the government, then joined Amway in 1977 as a secretary.

One evening, in a Kowloon restaurant overlooking Hong Kong island, she told me: "You should not interview me, my story is not important. What is important are the distributors' stories, because they are the ones who really turn these business opportunities into reality!"

If it is the distributors who must be credited for Amway's success, what is your role?

Eva Cheng: My role has been changing. I was able to grow with the company and widen my horizons. Now what I do best is manage. I manage relationships between World Headquarters, distributors, employees, business associates, the media or government officials. My job is to keep the balance between all those people. I can only say that I work with a devotion to the business, I am a serious worker and what I do, I want to do well.

But the status of Hong Kong will change in 1997.

Eva Cheng: Yes. In 1997, Hong Kong will become a special administrative region of the People's Republic of China. The future of Hong Kong is closely related to the developing trends in mainland China where major reforms are taking place. Although China is perceived as taking one step backward for every three steps forward, it is important to take a long-term view of the macro-trends. They are positive and show China making progress slowly but surely. While the Tien An Men Square incident was indeed a step backward, on the whole the country is making progress.

Hong Kong is a cultural melting pot. As we grew up, we were educated in Cantonese and English languages. Today most people in Hong Kong speak also Mandarin, the Chinese language spoken in Beijing.

If you consider trends over a period of ten to fifteen years, one has to be optimistic about China. People in China today accept the Communist Party leadership because it has adopted open-door economic reforms. Chinese are very pragmatic, not willing to give up political power, and so the political leadership will allow a degree of change without giving up political power. They have allowed a greater degree of individual enterprise. The Chinese people already have enjoyed the fruits of this open-door policy and will not give it up easily. If economic reforms were halted, I think the Chinese people would not accept it. The ruling party is intelligent and understands this. China, according to what I hear from inside sources, is at a major turning point in its history. The question is, at what pace?

Why did Amway choose the Guandong province to build its Chinese plant?

Eva Cheng: In the South, officials are more open to new ideas and concepts than those in the North. They are much more entrepreneurial. I have represented Amway in meetings with officials and negotiators. Lawyers, tax consultants from outside and from Ada were of great help. I am part of a team, I have very strong support from Ada. We started back in 1988 to negotiate or rather initiate discussions. Then, because of the events of Tien An Men Square, we shelved the project for one year before we started actively again. We signed an agreement in September 1992 and will start building a factory on 58,000 square meters in the Guangzhou Economic and Technological Development District. It will take from a year to a year and a half. Then we'll start building inventory and hiring staff. Dan DeVos came to the joint-venture contract signature ceremony on September 22. Dave Van Andel was at the ground-breaking ceremony the first week of November 1992.

When will Amway start to operate in China?

Eva Cheng: We hope to start in 1994. The factory will be 100 kilometers north of Hong Kong. Today 60 million people live within 100 miles of our new venture there. Our factory will be 12,000 square meters with a possible extension to 30,000. It is a much bigger project than in Korea and it will be the largest manufacturing facility outside Amway headquarters.

How fast will the business develop?

Eva Cheng: We do not know, but people in China are starving for opportunities! Avon entered China in 1989 and invested one million dollars. Today they have 10,000 distributors and expect to double to 20,000 within a year. Amway is making a major commitment with an initial investment of 29 million US dollars in Guandong.

I asked Eva Cheng how, after 15 years with Amway, she sees the company. "There are a lot of lessons we can learn from the other markets. The more I work for Amway, the more I realize that the sales force needs to be trained and disciplined and taught the rules of the game. We go through a learning curve and we learn through our failures as well as our successes.

The psyche of people is always difficult to evaluate. It is not inevitable that the distributors will get out of control, however it is inevitable that the distributors always demand more from the company as they become more mature. They want better quality, better systems of information.

In the States, Amway may have been too liberal; in Europe we're trying to tighten up. We tend to be much stricter in our rules enforcement, and we spend more time educating the Direct Distributors. It varies according to cultures and markets.

My experience is that, in our part of the world, distributors are basically reasonable people but very demanding. Asians have more respect for authority, they are more willing to discipline themselves, they are not so individualistic. Look at a Chinese family at dinner where everybody shares the plates. In Europe, you order your own food and you eat from your own plate. In Asia, we do not have the problem of distributors who use religious overtones or sell books or tapes about direct selling or self-development, instead of selling Amway products.

It is clear that we must stimulate freedom, but at the same time we must have the courage to direct the way that freedom is expressed so that the common interest is protected.

The auto-dynamics of direct selling are bound to get out of control easily. The balance between freedom and control is not easy to strike. Sometimes the pendulum swings too heavily to one side or the other. I think today, after 34 years of operation, Amway has a better sense of what needs to be done."

Taiwan

Eva Cheng is also Managing Director for Taiwan, a market of 20 million people with an annual per capita revenue of NT$10,000. With more than 50,000 distributors and a staff of 180 people, Amway's Taiwan business approximates US$150–180 million.

On staff is Pitos Puong, who came from Phnom Penh, Cambodia in 1981 and, after receiving his law degree, joined Amway Taiwan. As he told me one day in Tokyo, Amway's Taiwan entry was difficult because some companies had practiced pyramid schemes and so multi-level marketing had a bad image. But today, the government has issued legislation and Amway is well received and growing very fast.

Malaysia

On August 13, 1992, some 300 local Amway Distributors met at the Hilton Hotel in Kuala Lumpur, Malaysia, to share their experiences, hear about new products and meet with Choong Lai Huat, Managing Director of Amway Malaysia, Indonesia, and Thailand. That evening I was introduced to a few of the 27 Diamond Distributors operating from Malaysia which has three principal communities: Malaysian, Chinese and Indian. That means three languages are used on a day-to-day basis, plus English. In Kuala Lumpur, all meetings are held in English. In more rural areas, Malaysian or

Chinese is used. Each month, three different language editions of the *AMAGRAM* magazine are published.

That evening, most of the Diamond Direct Distributors were deeply involved in international sponsoring. As Nortrini Bt Yacob pointed out, "We go to Indonesia or Australia to develop our business." For Anisah Bt A Razak whose main activity is teaching college, Amway takes most of his free time." My wife is in Jakarta for two weeks to build up the network I sponsored in Mexico, Canada and Taiwan. We meet a lot of competition. The Amway opportunity looks simple, but it is complex and you have to think a lot about it!"

Gladstone and Violet Pereira qualified as Diamonds in 1989. Their network extends to Australia, Taiwan and Indonesia. As Gladstone says, "Amway is really a family business." In fact, he has 11 brothers and sisters, and eight of them are distributors!

Managing Director of Amway Malaysia is L. H. Choong. A graduate from Malaysia University, he joined the company in 1978, after working with ESSO, Kimberly Clark and Colgate.

"This business is a people business. Like tonight at the Hilton, we bring people together, we laugh together and we discuss problems. We build people and people know how to build business. The idea is to maximize human resources.

The uniqueness of this business is that people come from all origins. When we started, most people came to us in slippers, and today they are all well dressed. I remember one who was working in a factory in very bad conditions. He did not speak a word of English, nor Chinese, and he is now Diamond!

Distributors succeed because they are persistent in the beginning, during those years when you do not make much money. Their motivation? Challenge, fun, friends, independence, willingness to persist or any other personal objectives.

In Europe, affluence and leisure are more important. Here people tend to take work more seriously. Do not think that here it is easier to sell to a relative. First you have to be successful on your own. The only reason the family comes in is because they see success is possible. The family helps only to solidify the business".

Choong Lai Huat, with the help of Low Han-Kee and Alice Yeoh, Public Relations Executive, developed Amway sponsorship of a great number of social and community projects. This helped to enhance the company's image in countries where direct selling was often compared to or confused with illegal pyramid schemes.

Amway Malaysia started its operations in 1976 with five employees in a modest rented shop. Since then, it has grown steadily and moved to its own 60,000 square foot building. It has a staff of more than 200, and an active distributor force of over 40,000. It is a very profitable affiliate of Amway Corporation. It is very similar to Thailand which has 200,000 distributors, a staff of 200 and where 60 percent of the business originated from Malaysia leaders.

One of the best ideas implemented by Choong was to sell insurance contracts in Malaysia through the Amway network. "We wanted to find a way to reach the working people in the countryside. We created a master plan with the help of an insurance company, Jerneh

Insurance, and we propose that people join the plan." The Amsure personal accident insurance plan was launched in January 1989. More than 10,000 people signed up within three months of the launch. The Amsure plan includes 24-hour insurance coverage worldwide for death and permanent disablement. Amway and Jerneh Insurance made the commitment to pay out all the claims within one month. In two years, Amway Malaysia sold 130,000 insurance policies, a success which has led to ideas about distribution of other financial services.

A cross-cultural distributor

Foo, an overseas Chinese, was born in Malaysia. After receiving his bachelor's degree from a Malaysian university, he worked in a chemical company as a sales representative. He started his Amway business in 1978 when Amway Malaysia opened. He started with much hesitation and little confidence. His goal was to accumulate some capital so that he could go into business later. But, after attending a meeting held by his upline Direct Distributor, Gerald and Angela De Silva, he revised his thinking. "That was my turning point. I began to see the overwhelming potential of the business and decided to commit myself to making it a success," he said.

Foo worked hard and committed himself to the Amway business as a long-term business. In three years, he became Diamond Direct Distributor in Malaysia. His success in Malaysia encouraged him to build a second business in Taiwan. With his experience, his strong belief in the Amway Sales and Marketing Plan, his contagious honest personality, his adventurous spirit, and an enormous appetite for hard work, he foresaw his success in Taiwan. As he said at a rally, "Some people told me that as an overseas Chinese, it would be difficult to start the Amway business in a country unknown to me, without friends and relatives. But when I stepped off the airplane, I saw a lot of people in the streets and I was excited. "There is a big opportunity here," I told myself, "because it is a people's business."

Foo is a well-organized and goal-oriented person. But he is also known as an honest person and one who follows the Amway Rules of Conduct to the letter. He firmly believes and preaches that one must not exaggerate the income potential of the Amway Sales and Marketing Plan, or over-claim the quality of products. It is only through respect for customers and prospects and honesty with downline distributors that one can build a long-term business. Foo became Double Diamond Direct Distributor in Taiwan in 1986, five years after the market started. In 1987, when Amway Thailand opened, he started to build his third overseas business. In 1991, he became Diamond Direct Distributor there. In 1993, he is Diamond in three countries, Malaysia, Taiwan and Thailand. Foo has at least 30 Direct Distributor "legs" (Amway jargon for downline groups) in all three markets, and distributors traceable to him are counted by the tens of thousands. In July 1992, when Amway Indonesia opened, Foo began his fourth business.

Thailand

Preecha Prakobkit, General Manager for Thailand, likes to say, "The secret of Amway's success is the free enterprise spirit. We are a model of direct selling through networking. The network system in the long run is more stable than the single direct system which is administratively faster, but cannot be expanded as easily. In Amway's network, if one distributor gives up, others continue to service our clients."

Training distributors is a key factor of success. In one year, Amway Thailand organizes some 300 different three-day training courses all over the country. "Amway distributors pass on what they get from training to other distributors because everyone benefits when others are able to sell."

Korea

In Korea, the company has faced a lot of problems in spite, or because, of its success. The Korean Ministry of Finance issued Amway a business license in 1987 with the condition that Amway would "help Korea develop new technologies, improve the quality of similar products made in Korea and in turn benefit Korean consumers." In 1990 Amway built a factory in Eumsung, Choong-buk Province. In 1991 Amway Korea was established. In less than a year, 48,000 Koreans had signed up as distributors.

This is what *BUSINESS AND INDUSTRY* magazine
(February 1992), published in Korea, reports:

"Amway Corporation is discovering what other
foreign companies operating here have long known:
grey areas in commercial law, combined with the
interpretive whims of government bureaucrats, can
make doing business in Korea difficult. In less than a
year, Amway's enormous success on the Korean
market has raised the ire of powerful local
competitors bent on curbing the company's competitive clout . . . .

Korea's rigid Confucian hierarchy could provide
the government with its best excuse for intervention.
Consumers in the United States may be relatively
free to decide for themselves whether or not to join
the Amway family. But in Korea, Confucian norms
can make it difficult for someone of lower rank to
resist invitations of sponsorship from someone of
higher rank. Those at the bottom of the hierarchy
may be under the greatest pressure to buy and – at
the same time – in the least favourable position to
sell . . . Korean officials argue that multi-level
marketing is not geared to Korean society. But it is
and that's the problem."

A similar judgment appeared the month before (January
1992) in *KOREA TODAY*: "Amway's success here in
Korea is partly attributed to the fact that its sales system
matches well with the local custom that Koreans maintain
a close relationship with relatives or schoolmates."

Australia

Today, Amway Australia, with a turnover of A$250 million, is the country's largest direct selling company. More than 100,000 distributors sell 2,500 products. Bruce Shankland, who became Managing Director for Europe in 1993, says that a growing number of manufacturers and suppliers are being drawn to direct selling operations. "We are buying products from companies that two or three years ago were reluctant to deal with direct selling firms. They were almost scared of upsetting the traditional retailers. But they are no longer scared. In Australia, direct selling is a big growth area in the retail industry and suppliers see it as an efficient, economical way of moving their goods into the marketplace." Thirty percent of the products sold by Amway Australia come from local suppliers, the rest from Amway factories in the US, Europe and Asia.

Amway's rallies in Melbourne regularly attract up to 15,000 present and prospective distributors, which is why Amway considers it a reasonable goal to have 200,000 distributors and annual sales of $1 billion by 1999.

Interviewed about distributors' incomes, Bruce Shankland said, "Many, of course, earn very large incomes, however, it is company policy to undersell rather than oversell the benefits of the Amway business opportunity. Some networks have retail sales well in excess of A$10 million."

But Amway Australia didn't start as a success. It started as a challenge which Rich DeVos decided to face by trying out his company overseas for the first time. Amway arrived with a very small staff . . . and six products!

To head this pioneer expedition, DeVos chose Bill Hemmer who, you might say, knew Amway inside and out. He had started as an Amway employee in 1967, then, a few years later, had left the company to become an independent distributor for a short time. When he finally decided he preferred the corporate opportunity, he returned to Amway and was sent to Australia in 1971.

Why Australia?

Bill Hemmer: The idea was to see whether the Amway Sales and Marketing Plan, our method of selling products and recruiting people into the multi-level mass merchandising program was an exportable commodity. Until then, we had never really proved it could go beyond the borders of the United States and Canada, which is a different country, of course, but has a lot of similarities with the States.

Did you feel confident moving into Australia?

Bill Hemmer: I remember what Rich DeVos said: 'If it doesn't work, we can always come home if we're too embarrassed.'

You didn't come home, though.

Bill Hemmer: We had a lot of problems, but we persevered. And we proved Amway is exportable.

Since opening the Australian frontier, you have worked in Japan. Did you find the same problems as in Australia? Could you implement the same marketing plan, the same culture of business as in Australia?

Bill Hemmer: The situation is very, very similar the world over, including Japan. If you take distributors from every country we operate in and put them all in the same room and if you couldn't see their faces or know what nationality they are, you would think they are all from the same place. Of course, some might be more enthusiastic, some less. Some might work harder because culturally . . As you know, the Japanese take very little vacation, the French are accustomed to five weeks and the Germans to six . . . Those differences exist, but people's basic wants and needs are the same the world over. That's what we started to discover in Australia and what we have proved over and over again.

10

South America

As far as Amway is concerned, South America was discovered by Steve Robbins. A lawyer before joining the company, fluent in French, Spanish and Portuguese, he opened the Amway markets of Panama, Guatemala, Brazil and Argentina. Robbins, with his pioneer spirit and communicative ways, smooths the way each time, then calls for an Amway manager to run the new headquarters.

Guatemala

Steve Robbins opened headquarters here in September 1987, then General Manager Rob Davidson was appointed. When asked why Amway chose Guatemala, Davidson said: "After our success in Panama, Guatemala seemed the next best 'stepping stone' in Latin America. Mexico and Brazil were just too big for us at the time. El Salvador and Nicaragua had bad political problems and Costa Rica very tight economic controls. But Guatemala had just changed from a military dictatorship to a free enterprise system encouraging foreign investment. Also, the socio-cultural aspects of Guatemalan family structure really lent itself to our networking system."

What problems did you face?

Rob Davidson: The business environment made it difficult for us to find suitable commercial property and building wasn't possible then either. So we started in a house in a residential area. There was also an infrastructure problem once business began to grow beyond Guatemala City.

How did you solve it?

Rob Davidson: We set up a pick-up center in Jutiapa because the distributor population was growing fast there. Then we bought a truck to carry the products out to the center.

Inflation was very high in Guatemala, I believe. Did it affect your operations?

Rob Davidson: It was Amway's first experience in a country with high inflation. So we laid the ground for greater price flexibility. Previously, our prices were raised annually, but today, in Guatemala and in Brazil too, we make price adjustments much more frequently. Since Guatemala was one of the first Third World markets Amway entered, we also had another problem concerning product pricing. Our products often weren't affordable because they were packaged in large sizes. So we developed a "bolsita" with SA8, a laundry detergent.

We opened workshops employing handicapped people who repackaged it from one large package into 33 small bags, each to be used on a single laundry load. By doing this, we also solved another problem. People were using far too much of the product, which is concentrated (as are many Amway products), because they didn't or couldn't read the instructions. Making one-dose packages made the "cost per use" message clear and provided us with one of many valuable lessons for later market entries into Mexico and Brazil.

Mexico

Amway came to Mexico in June 1990, soon after President Carlos Salinas de Gortari's government liberalized controls and began to welcome foreign investment. Russ Hall, Amway's Regional Manager for Mexico, Brazil, Panama and Guatemala, had to face the challenge of functioning in a country with an extremely weak infrastructure. Here are just a few examples:

- The postal system and parcel delivery service were haphazard . . . when they functioned at all.

- The banking system was far from modern.

- The strict regionalization of Mexico meant that people in a given area had access only to goods manufactured locally, unless they were willing and able to travel great distances.

What did Amway do to solve these problems? Russ Hall and his staff decided to innovate by treating the whole of Mexico as a single marketplace. In collaboration with a privately-owned local company that made parcel deliveries, they developed Mexico's first system of home delivery. To improve telephone operations, they installed one of Mexico's first fiber-optics systems and they also pioneered the use of credit cards in telemarketing.

Following the Guatemalan example, they created 15 pick-up centers to make goods rapidly available. Today 70 percent of all sales are made at these centers.

In short, not only did they lay the grounds for successful Amway businesses, but they considerably modernized the country which had opened its doors to them.

But when Amway came to Mexico, it found more than a series of obstacles to be hurdled. It also found a population very attracted by American goods (Mexicans spend 13 percent of their disposable income on them), and by Amway's spirit of free enterprise. The Salinas administration was highly interested in the world market, had increased imports by 20 percent and was already heading toward the US–Mexico Free Trade Agreement.

Brazil

Steve Robbins started thinking about Brazil in 1985 when he was involved in launching Amway in Panama and Guatemala. His original strategy had been to open a "pilot" market in Panama and then establish a priority list of market entries based on criteria such as size, demographics, economic conditions, local currency convertibility, legislation, tax factors, and so on. Brazil was high on the list, largely because of the proven success of direct selling activities (Avon, present since the early 1970s, was a large and profitable business). Robbins had been informed that most cosmetics were sold in Brazil through direct selling channels. The principal negative factor was the prohibition of non-essential imports. This meant that Amway would have had to produce all its products locally.

Between 1987 and 1990 efforts were made to secure government approval of a number of locally-sourced homecare and personal care products for a planned launch in October 1990. However, owing to import prohibition and high local taxation which reduced net profitability below Amway's international standards, the project did not receive approval from Amway's head-quarters. But investment conditions started changing in Brazil with the election of Fernando Collor de Mello. His business-oriented policies included import liberal-ization. It became appropriate to rewrite Amway's investment project on the basis of 100 percent imports from Ada, Michigan. This new project was approved and the Brazil launch was scheduled for November 1991.

Amway opened its headquarters in Sao Paulo. Over 600 international Amway distributors from around the world (principally the USA and Australia) participated. 11,000 starter kits were distributed within the first few days and almost 60,000 in the first 10 months. By the end of September 1992, Amway Brazil Ltd had a distributor force of 38,000 with monthly sales reaching almost US$ 900,000. For the first time in a new international market, Amway's complete skin care and cosmetics line (118 items) was introduced, plus a 16-piece cookware set and three homecare items. Ten months later, Amway had added another seven products, principally homecare.

If Amway is developing so fast today in Brazil, it is mainly thanks to international distributors. As Robbin says, "One of the major reasons for the successful launch was the action by the international groups of sponsorship. When I was in France, these internationally oriented distributors were becoming a powerful and significant force in the opening of new Amway markets. They had an ability to organize and plan comparable to that of Amway itself. Rather than arriving in a new market as individual distributors operating in a purely autonomous fashion, five or six major international groups were now preparing in advance for the launch. Able to virtually guarantee a successful launch in terms of starter kit sales and new recruits, these international lines of sponsorship are becoming powerful vehicles for expansion of international businesses. They modify the face of new market development for the company."

It is too soon to draw conclusions about Amway's contribution to the Brazilian economy, but some trends are apparent. As in other markets, Amway acts as a catalyst for change. Amway is "first world" and offers to its distributors first-world treatment. In Brazil, this means toll-free ordering with direct debits to their bank accounts. This obviates the need to place a written order and go to the bank to effect payment (checks are not sent via mail in Brazil, nor in many other Latin countries). Amway is thus able to process and ship orders in record-breaking time.

As Steve Robbins says, "In Brazil, Amway goes where the distributors are. Because they are in the largest centers of population, we opened three pick-up centers (PUCs) in Sao Paulo and one in Rio when we launched. New PUCs are now being prepared in Brasilia and Curitiba and additional ones are programmed for Belo Horizonte and Campinas where distributor activities and growth potential are strong."

Are there also cultural reasons to be so optimistic?

Steve Robbins: Definitely. One characteristic which Brazilians and Argentinians share is a thirst for the opportunity which an entrepreneurial company like Amway offers. Latins in these countries have been, and still are, precluded from initiating small individual enterprises by the seemingly insurmountable bureaucratic and cultural hurdles. Amway is large and steadfast enough and has sufficient resources to overcome the inertia opposing individual effort and innovation: Amway's principal contribution is that it makes it possible for the individual to achieve something otherwise unimaginable – owning his own business without exhausting himself and his resources in the process.

Amway's staff in both Brazil and Argentina intuitively understand and flourish within this new cultural orientation. Extremely competent and hard-working individuals in both countries make up our management. They appear to find in Amway an ideal environment for their own growth and contributions.

While Amway can be expected to prosper wherever men and women are allowed to exercise their own initiative, caution must still be applied. The current political and economic scenes throughout Latin America are generally propitious for Amway's entry but the possibility of change, often of an unforeseeable or violent type, must be calculated into business strategies. I would say that Amway's future in Latin America is brilliant and assured; there will, however, still be the same (if not somewhat larger!) pitfalls and obstacles as in any new venture to be overcome. The rewards, however, should certainly justify the effort.

Argentina

When I corresponded with Steve Robbins, he and his staff were preparing the launch of Amway Argentina, due to open by March 1993 with seven homecare and three personal care products. I asked him what his expectations were.

Steve Robbins: Although the population of Argentina, 34 million, is significantly smaller than that of Brazil, 145 million, our sales and distributors' recruiting expectations are not proportionately reduced. We should have no fewer than 35,000 distributors in the initial 12-month period.

Why such high hopes?

Steve Robbins: First of all, Argentina is perhaps unique in Latin America with its highly Europeanized population and one of the smallest, if not the smallest, percentage of indigenous peoples.

Like Chile and Mexico before it, Argentina is currently committed to reversing its posture as a state-controlled or dominated megalithic entity in favor of a market-driven economy. Carlos Saul Menem, the President, and his Minister of Economy, Domingo Cavallo, while ostensibly from Peronist molds, have, in fact, made enormous progress in liberalizing the economy and restoring private initiative. Such changes bode well for Amway in so far as finished consumer goods are once again permitted at reasonable duty rates (averaging 22 percent), the Argentine peso and the dollar are at parity and freely convertible and private enterprise is increasingly encouraged.

11

Communicating

To answer the specific and extremely complex needs of a company present in over 50 countries and territories and including approximately two million private businesses, each different from the other, Amway has conceived and built state-of-the-art information systems. Among their myriad tasks, they must support the Sales and Marketing Plan worldwide, simplify each distributor's business, track business activity in all its multiple functions and adapt to a constantly evolving and expanding company.

In March 1992, Amway finalized a Strategic Information Plan which will be followed until 1995. It will support Amway's intention to open four new markets per year and its assumption that existing markets will continue to grow at more than ten percent per year. It will ensure that the interface to distributors is consistent across markets that have different regulations, cultures, standards of living, infrastructures, market opportunities, competitive threats and technology. It will transmit standards for business processes established at Ada and allow affiliate management to operate within these standards while adapting the Amway business to local conditions.

The Strategic Information Plan calls for a new, automated way of developing and maintaining business applications, and for the renewal of the core business application portfolio. The hardware and operating software platform will continue to be carefully controlled worldwide, to benefit from shared skills. This process makes all markets as similar as possible, while allowing the differences necessary to satisfy regulations and management direction.

Among key data items are information about distributors, sales, bonuses, finance, personnel and inventory (daily transfer of inventory movements is imperative). Marketing data for planning future products is another key factor.

In addition to data, procedures associated with the processing and transmission of data must be specified by World Headquarters in Ada and transmitted to all affiliates. This is one reason that worldwide computerization is a requirement at Amway.

Today, Amway is in the excellent position of using a relatively small number of hardware/software platforms, compared with other companies. An IBM mainframe computer is used at the headquarters in Ada, and most affiliates run their businesses on IBM AS/400 minicomputers. Amway has about 30 installed today, and each new market is receiving one. Amway's communication facilities are extremely advanced. IBM confirms that Amway has the most sophisticated AS/400 network in Europe today.

Japan

Particularly interesting because of its huge market potential, Amway Japan has already outgrown its AS/ 400 platform and has added an IBM mainframe. Its team for Information Technology Strategy (ITS), which has a staff of 31, provides for regular communication with World Headquarters in Ada to ensure integrity of data definition and the protection of core business processes. ITS complements and enhances global information strategy by calling for application development in support of markets beyond Japan. All systems handle multiple languages in addition to Japanese and English. The total cost of the ITS function at Amway Japan over the next five years will be about $US 80 million.

Europe

Jim Robins was in charge of Amway computer systems in Europe up to end 1992, and based at the German affiliate. He started at Amway Canada in 1979 and came to Europe in November 1990, just when the Spanish and German markets were booming. In fact, they had grown too fast, with hundreds of thousands of new distributors signed in a very short time, and Amway's systems, staff and computer equipment could no longer keep up with them. Soon after Robins' arrival, he was faced with Amway Germany's move from Germering to Puchheim, north of Munich. "It was a frightening move because on one weekend we had to take two computers and all of our communications lines for Europe and relocate them to another place. But it went along almost perfectly. Inventory, payment of bonus, distributor records, everything had to be moved almost overnight for all countries in Europe, that meant for about 500,000 distributors."

He told me Amway had to face considerable problems in Spain too. "In June 1991, Amway installed a stand-alone computer in Spain because communications between Germany and Spain had become impossible; the lines would disconnect ten times a day. A second communication line had been ordered from the PTT in Spain in March 1991, but installed only in February 1992, 11 months later! That was the reality in Spain in 1991. Amway sent its best programmers to Barcelona for four months, recabled its building there and tried everything it could before making the decision to have a stand-alone computer and spend one million dollars on it. A bigger computer was also installed in Italy and in London, and a small computer was put in each of the Product Selection Centers in Germany, Austria and Hungary."

What about Eastern Europe?

Jim Robins: In the east of Germany in 1991, the distributors kept coming and Amway could not service them properly because of communication problems. The telephones did not work, so the distributors could not be registered and it was very difficult to run the inventory. In the meantime, Amway started to investigate satellite communications and installed satellite dishes in March 1992 so the Munich office could communicate with all the Amway computers in Europe. With a dish in Hanover, information gets to satellite and then to each Product Service Center. It goes about 23,000 miles in about half a second. At the end of 1992 all PSCs were able to communicate with Munich through satellite. Information is also sent by electronic mail to each of the 28 Amway international affiliate operations in two to three seconds. The whole world of Amway is today a huge communication network.

Building it must have been very complicated and difficult.

Jim Robins: To say the least! Take the example of Poland. The postal authorities there do not allow satellite dishes. So we have two options: (1) ordering a stand-alone computer or (2) ordering a lease line and satellite dishes. Finally we did both to see which solution worked better. The same problem arose in Portugal when we opened there in April 1992. A lease line was ordered, but also a backup line. Before going into a new country, Amway now experiments with different ways to ensure that all services will be covered.

The specifics of each country must be taken into account, as Robins pointed out. "The processing in Italy for example is a lot different from the processing in France because of the regulations of the countries. In Italy, there are four or five classes of distributors, so the structure of the marketing plan is different. There are different qualification levels, different currencies. In

Austria, the government says you must sell to the customer and use the distributor as an agent. In Germany, Amway must deal directly with each distributor by law. In the UK, only certain types of distributors are allowed to place orders. Every country is different."

That explains why Amway Europe has 11 different distributor records systems, 11 bonus systems, 11 inventory systems. When software has to be changed, it is changed 11 times. In early 1993, there were 38 programmers working in different countries of Amway. They all take directions from our German based EDP centre and travel from one country to another when needed. In Munich alone, there are 17 people in the computer room.

With so much to lose, security, of course, is taken very seriously. Amway backs up its files daily, weekly, monthly and yearly. It also has an agreement with IBM which can truck a computer to Munich within 24 hours in case of emergency.

Responsible for all information systems in Europe, Robins, I learned, had a straight-line relationship to Stewart McArthur at the London based European headquarters, and a dotted-line relationship to the US systems group in Michigan. He also reported to all the General Managers in each of the countries. "I have at least 13 bosses right now. My job is to build the information systems image for all Europe."

In France, distributors use Minitel from their home and can get their bonus or PV/BV information right away. Minitel interfaces with the Paris office which interfaces with Amway in Munich to get instant information. It is the same in Italy and Spain. Since December 1992, sales information is given by a voice-activated system, 24 hours a day, seven days a week. On-line applications, satellite communications, and voice systems make business in the world of Amway exciting, innovative and proactive for all distributors, in whatever countries they operate.

Japan stands on its own, communicates with the US, but does not support any other market, just like Spain or Australia. Australia has a unique type of order entry system, like Minitel in France. Videotel in Italy is also unique. Amway is installing Evotel in Spain, which again will be unique. It will function within the existing telecommunications structure, but it can never be made standard. Since local legislation brings immediate changes, like the value-added tax in Spain, the company must be extremely well informed, on a day-to-day basis, about what is happening in each country. As Robins pointed out, "The computer is at the heart of our company. If it does not work, the company does not work. You can take the Sales department and send them away for two or three months and the business will continue to run. It might not grow, but it will continue to run. If the computer department is sent away for a day, everything stops completely."

Language is also an important communications problem. "I speak only English," said Robins, "and people in a lot of countries will say that they speak English. Well, they may understand it, but some do not really speak English. If you are on the telephone to somebody in Spain, and you say something three times, it may not happen the way you want it to happen.

Sometimes it is a question of verb tense. They do not know whether you said: I want to do this today, in the future or I did it yesterday."

I asked Jim Robins about his previous professional experience and how it compared with working at Amway. He told me he worked for 11 years in Canada for an insurance company.

"Insurance was very conservative, relaxed and predictable. Before launching a new insurance product, you have at least a year to make the programming changes. But Amway is different. We constantly must be on-line; information must be available on a day-to-day basis. Things are happening all the time. Government decisions, distributors' wants and needs change constantly. And of course the company is constantly launching new products, opening new markets. Just imagine Mercedes Benz or any other company trying to go into four new countries a year, which is Amway's goal. It's not so easy! Especially now that all the 'good' countries are gone. It is very hard to find people who want to live in Warsaw, for example, who speak Polish and who have the kind of experience we're looking for."

After three years in Munich, Jim Robins returned to the US in 1993 to work in the International Department. "We advertised to find my successor here. We want a German national or a European who speaks German. Initially we had a largely English-speaking staff "club" here, which was one reason there was some resentment about Amway's presence at first. I guess they thought we were trying to take over, but I hope by now we've proved we are here to be helpful and that when we leave, we prefer to hire German people to replace us."

Amway communicates through a vast computer galaxy which allows it to manage and expand its business in over 50 countries and territories. But for this company whose success depends on highly motivated distributors, communication also means enormous, ultra-modern printing capacities which turn out tens of millions of magazines, brochures and newsletters each year. The machinery and the personnel required to create these publications are extremely costly but have proved to be an excellent investment. If Amway is by far the world's most profitable homecare and personal care company, it is not only because of its products and its marketing plan or its computerized information network but thanks to the powerful motivating force of its internal communications.

12

Amway Is Only Human

Amway is certainly one of the most "human" companies in the world . . . which is one way of saying that it is not perfect, at least in the eyes of some outside observers. Over the years, it has inspired much skepticism and been criticized for some of its most basic principles. In the spirit of impartial reporting, I would like to summarize a few of these negative reactions and let the reader be the judge.

Free enterprise. Amway is based on the great American principle of free enterprise, but some critics maintain that if Amway entrepreneurs are free, their customers are not. They say they are victims of "forced selling." Even if, officially, there is no purchase obligation, people order, not because they really want the products but because, as guests of the distributor who has invited them to his or her home, they feel obliged to "return the favor."

But criticism of taking advantage of their guests' politeness is mild in comparison to the accusation of outright manipulation. Experienced distributors, who have become experts in psychology, purportedly dissimulate their real and sole objective which is to make a sale and exercise their subtle domination over weak or naive prospects. Amway's critics believe that all forms of selling, including the friendly, low-key Amway method, are uniquely profit-oriented.

Free time. This criticism expresses concern about the distributors themselves. A great many start their businesses in their free time and, justifiably, are delighted to use it in such a fruitful way at first. But as often happens, the more time they devote to Amway, the more successful – and motivated – they become. Eventually all their time is spent building networks, counselling their own distributors, organizing meetings and assuming responsibility for more and more people who count on their leadership. Completely absorbed in their profitable group activity, they can evolve as individuals only *within* the Amway family. They cannot discover or pursue enriching cultural or artistic or leisure activities which are not part of Amway's vast motivational program. They cannot devote themselves to people who are not part of the Amway network. Last, but far from least, they have neither the time nor the perspective to question whether their total commitment to Amway is not just a way of escaping from certain personal problems and whether the self-esteem they feel does not depend entirely on their rank in the Amway hierarchy and would disappear in another context. For these reasons, critics say that if Amway can often broaden horizons, it can also narrow them.

Positive thinking. To just about everybody, at first glance "positive" is good and "negative" is bad. So why does the Amway attitude of positive thinking inspire skepticism and sometimes even hostility?

Although it is certainly true that, as a salesman, you must know what result you want to attain and you must believe you can succeed in order to do so, reality is more complicated than that. It is full of examples of people who use their positive image of themselves and their goals to overpower others. How many have gained prestige and privileges neither through their good work nor their intelligence, but because their profit-sharing project fills their pockets with the fruit of other people's efforts?

Positive thinking also has some controversial social and political connotations. The idea that you can succeed if you really want to easily leads to the conclusion that people who are unemployed, or surviving at the poverty level, simply do not want to change their situations – an opinion liberal observers abhor and combat.

Togetherness. The Amway family has often been criticized for the style of its rallies where thousands of people are brought together to celebrate their success, but seem to be in the throes of religious or political fervour. This massive grouping of like-thinking people has led critics to suspect that Amway may exclude people who do not share certain fundamentalist or conservative views, or people who simply are not interested in fitting into a crowd. These rallies also raise the question of the bonding power of crowds where the momentary satisfaction of belonging can lead some to make long-term engagements they may regret once the party is over.

The good life. Top Amway achievers are rewarded by the thunderous applause of their colleagues, but also with high cash bonuses, luxury cruises and vacations at exotic resort hotels. With their earnings, they often buy the most expensive cars, private planes and vast estates. This display of wealth which, by Amway standards, seems to epitomize "the good life", is often mocked by those who believe that money isn't everything, that success is subjective and achievement an inner, spiritual value. They quote the popular expression "Living well is the best revenge" to suggest that the accumulation and display of material wealth is just a way of compensating for the absence of more precious riches.

Women's rights. Thousands of prosperous Amway businesses were started by married women. Only once their businesses showed promise did their husbands decide to participate in their spare time. Today the great majority of Amway distributors work in couples and are remunerated as such, although the women usually devote a great deal more time to the business than the husbands do. Some feminist critics believe that women should be paid their fair share of the couple's earnings.

Are these criticisms valid? Are they just the gripes of people envious of Amway's fabulous success? I hope this book will help you form your own opinion.

Rough sailing

Amway has grown so fast and so widely that many people see it as omnipotent and invulnerable. But over the years it has had to face a great many difficulties, some caused by national and economic obstacles, others by the weaknesses of human nature. Some examples are listed below.

- Amway has sometimes been the victim of its most fervent members. In 1991, Procter and Gamble won a suit against Amway distributors for spreading rumors that P&G and its products were instruments of Satan! Rich DeVos explained: "When you deal with over a million people, you are going to have some who overstep boundaries." It must be remembered that distributors are not Amway employees, but independent business people who are not screened before becoming part of the Amway family and are not controlled afterwards.

- Some distributors, over the years, have taken advantage of Amway's name and prestige to peddle unauthorized products or training programmes to their customers or recruits. When Amway discovers these practices and if they do not come to an end, the distributorships are discontinued, even when Amway loses giant, high-income networks in the process, as it has in several countries.

- Amway opened headquarters in Japan in 1979, just after the direct selling laws were changed to clamp down on illegal pyramid schemes. Although a careful reading of the Sales and Marketing Plan shows that Amway is not a pyramid and that the newest distributor has the same chance his predecessors had, few people took the time to read it. As a result,

the Japan operation had a very slow and shaky
beginning.

- Amway's Hong Kong operation took ten years to
  make profits and see its first Direct Distributors. Just
  a few years later, the largest Diamond group of
  distributors started to sell competitors' products
  through the Amway network. Amway cancelled all
  their sponsorship rights and lost about ten percent of
  its Hong Kong business. But this decision strength-
  ened bonds between honest distributors and Amway.

- After initiating negotiations with the Chinese to open
  a plant in a Southern province, Amway shelved its
  project for over a year after the events at Tien An
  Men Square.

- When Amway entered Mexico after President Salinas
  liberalized controls, it discovered a country with
  archaic postal, telephone, banking and delivery
  systems. Amway had to find ways of improving
  these facilities – in collaboration with local entrepreneurs – before it could hope to function efficiently.

- International distributors were over-enthusiastic
  about entering the Polish and Indonesian markets
  before Amway was officially cleared to do business
  there. Some of them took their products with them,
  but did not register them correctly. They also
  neglected to translate labels and instructions and so
  local consumers could not use them properly and

Amway's image suffered considerably before the market was officially "open for business."

- In Austria, zealous distributors started selling Amway products before the company officially opened with a solid infrastructure in place. This improper activity obliged Amway to delay its launch date by two years.

My 12 convictions about Amway

I have studied the Amway distribution system for nearly 20 years. To gain first-hand knowledge for a book written in 1985 and for this one, I met several times with Amway's co-founders and managers all over the world. Not only have I learned a great deal about direct selling in the process, but I have acquired a certain number of convictions about how the company is run, its objectives, philosophy and ethics.

To my view, the Amway corporation is:

1 *Serious.* There is no room for amateurs or dilettantes in its managerial positions. Its marketing plan, its system of rewards for distributors, its products and rules of conduct are honest and keep their promises.

2 *People-minded.* It gives priority to human values in its policies of hiring, training and rewarding. Service-oriented, it has understood that caring for others is the best strategy for success.

3 *Intelligent.* Its complex structure was conceived by rigorous minds and warm hearts. It has succeeded because employees and distributors are treated with dignity and respect and a true community spirit prevails.

4 *Generous.* The Amway philosophy is based on shared experience, shared profits, helping and training others to succeed. Its generosity to "its own" extends to wide sponsoring of cultural and environmental causes.

5 *Well-organized.* Management is highly professional and well structured, but it is also flexible and therefore prepared to take advantage of all new opportunities for free enterprise.

6 *Self-developing.* Its direct selling methods offer people one of today's best opportunities to grow, to develop their own capacities – and discover unexpected ones. As its people develop, so does Amway.

7 *Committed.* Management at World Headquarters and in each affiliate is totally dedicated to offering the most opportunity to the largest number of people.

8 *Ethical.* Compassionate capitalism would not succeed without integrity and dedication to a highly ethical business code.

9 *Self-renewing.* The company is not a fixed entity; it is a process, a pattern of movement. Despite difficulties and persistent misunderstanding about

direct selling, its values and organizational principles remain intact.

10 *Global.* It is a boundaryless company which adapts to each country but maintains its global vision. By stimulating international sponsoring and relationships, it effaces national borders. It also functions as a "melting pot" for specialists in production, research, marketing and finance and for all members of the Amway family, whether they are managers, employees or distributors.

11 *Proactive.* Modern in its marketing plan, imaginative, incentive, Amway is constantly on the move. New markets, new products, new incentives, new managers, new distributors are the very stuff of its daily life.

12 *Stimulating.* An exemplary motivator, rewarding every personal investment of time and energy, it has opened new financial, social and amicable horizons to millions.

13

Adventures and Altruism

Amway is devoted to the success of its own "family" of employees and distributors. But its commitments do not end there. For over 30 years, Amway has been one of the foremost supporters of environmental, cultural and humanitarian causes throughout the world.

In 1989, UN Secretary General Javier Perez de Cuellar presented the United Nations Environment Programme's Award for Achievement to Jay Van Andel and Rich DeVos in recognition of Amway's "commitment to the cause of environmental protection and awareness and for its generous support and encouragement to young people to make the environment a priority concern." To date, only one other corporation in the world has ever received this award.

Jay Van Andel's and Rich DeVos' concern for the environment started long before it became a burning issue. Their very first Amway product, created in 1954, has always contained only biodegradable cleaning agents. Faithful to their principles, they went on to support some of the major environmental projects of the last decade.

One of these adventures was ICEWALK, the International North Pole Expedition. A team of eight explorers, led by Robert Swan of the United Kingdom, became the first men to walk to the North Pole. A dramatic example of the "You can do it!" Amway attitude, the ICEWALK expedition's objective was to prove the ever-increasing danger of pollution in the polar regions and to focus attention on the threat to the earth's environment caused by ozone-layer depletion.

Stimulated by the spirit of ICEWALK, Amway later supported other environmental initiatives including GLOBAL RELEAF, which encouraged people all over the world to plant 100 million trees, and MASTERS OF THE ARCTIC, an exhibition of the works of Inuit and circumpolar artists, sponsored by the Amway Environmental Foundation and first shown at the United Nations before going on a world tour.

An international company, Amway follows through on its principles all over the world. In Austria, the Amway Environment Foundation brings the company and its distributors together to support local projects such as tree-plantings and natural playgrounds for children. In Japan, the Amway Nature Center supports the prestigious Kiyosato Forum for conservation education and each year organizes a fund-raising campaign which has aided such important projects as the One-Sapling-Per-Person program in Malawi, Africa and the Izunuma-Uchinuma Nature Sanctuary in Japan. Recently Amway Japan donated 500 cherry trees from Washington DC to the Tokyo Metropolitan government. Amway Thailand has supported a reforestation project, a wild animal rescue center and a tree-planting day for underprivileged children in the Slum Kindergarten Improvement Programme.

Truly people-oriented, Amway encourages its distributors to use their sense of initiative in community projects. In the UK, Amway distributors have raised funds for the Stackpole Trust which assists the disabled. Amway Taiwan has assisted the Eden Welfare Fund, the Holy Word Children's Foundation and the first Children Development Foundation. Amway Malaysia supports "Seedling of Hope", a project which provides foster families and special homes for difficult children. Amway Australia sponsors the "Young Achiever of the Year", an award encouraging entrepreneurship among students.

In 1991, the Amway Corporation was among the largest private donors to aid programs for victims of the Bangladesh disasters, Kurdish refugees, orphanages in Romania, relief agencies in Poland and a hospital in the former Soviet Union specializing in the treatment of victims of the Chernobyl nuclear disaster.

Devoted to the protection of Nature and "the Family of Man," Amway is also a major sponsor of significant cultural and artistic activities throughout the world.

Its first important international endeavour, in 1992, was the "Four American Artists" exhibition at the Stedelijk Museum in Amsterdam. At about the same time, it sponsored the European tour of the National Symphony Orchestra conducted by Mstislav Rostropovich. Both sponsorships were part of the Netherlands American Bicentennial of which Amway co-founder Jay Van Andel was the United States Commission Chairman.

The following years, Amway sponsored many other prestigious programmes in Europe. Among them were: the Gustav Mahler Youth Orchestra under the direction of Claudio Abbado; the Camerata Academica of the Mozarteum Salzburg under Sandor Vegh; the International Organ Competition at the Cathedral of Chartres; and the historic "homecoming" performance in Budapest of Sir Georg Solti and the Chicago Symphony Orchestra.

In the Asia/Pacific region, Amway played a major role in developing suburban Sydney's Hills Centre for the Performing Arts, and funded its huge ceramic mural by local artist Vladimir Tichy. In Hong Kong, it sponsored the tour of the Cleveland Orchestra conducted by Christoph Von Dohnanyi. In Japan, Amway proved to be a leading patron of the arts, sponsoring, among many other cultural events, the eight-city tour of the Bejart Ballet Lausanne, and performances by the Philadelphia Orchestra under Riccardo Muti and by the Cleveland Orchestra. Amway Japan was also responsible for the show at Tokyo's Hara Museum of the works of California artist Richard Diebenkorn and "Beyond the Frame: American Art 1960–1990", an exhibition shown in Tokyo's Setagaya Museum, Osaka's National Museum and Fukuoka's City Museum.

Over the years, the Amway Corporation and its distributors have been instrumental in dozens of environmental, cultural and humanitarian endeavours. But why did Amway choose those particular projects among the thousands of worthy causes in the world? To answer this question, one must keep in mind that, however sincerely generous and community-minded

Amway really is, it is not by vocation a philanthropic organization. It is a corporation which must give first consideration to its own profits and its corporate image.

Patronage of the arts

Private patronage of the arts has existed for centuries. During the Renaissance, for example, the Medicis became the leading art patrons of their day, and perhaps of all time, supporting some of the greatest artists the world has ever known.

Not until very recent times, however, did private enterprises become regularly involved in "corporate sponsorship." A corporate sponsorship which can be extended to many areas – sports, culture, charities, education – seeks to bring worthwhile human endeavours to the public in such a way that the image of the sponsored activity is linked with the corporation. Ideally this linkage should lead to a positive perception of the company. In other words, the public's good feeling about the sponsored event or organization is transferred to the sponsor.

Amway Japan, for example, proposed to fund tours of the Cleveland Orchestra and the San Francisco Symphony Orchestra because these projects fulfilled its three major objectives for sponsorship:

1   to positively profile Amway's image in society;

2   to develop and/or solidify necessary VIP contacts;

3   to generate pride in Amway and motivate their employees and distributors.

Clearly, the press coverage, advertising and promotional support of the concerts had a positive rub-off on Amway and its corporate image. The concerts also provided the opportunity for receptions where Amway managers could meet and communicate with key social and political figures who might directly or indirectly interact with the business. Although not immediately obvious, the goodwill generated can and does have long-term impact.

A sponsor obtains *external* benefits from building its corporate image, but also *internal* benefits, such as the positive feeling generated among employees and distributors, proud to be associated with such high-level activities. Art sponsorship can even be a useful recruitment tool, attracting quality employees and distributors who might not have been familiar with the company otherwise (Amway Japan often features sponsored cultural activities in its recruitment literature).

Although Amway sponsorship to date has focused on the performing arts, several visual arts projects have also been funded. When "Beyond the Frame: American Art 1960–1990" was proposed to Amway Japan management, a comparative study of the advantages of performing and visual arts was made:

• Advantages of Performing Arts Sponsorships:

1   Prestigious, traditional area of corporate support
2   Safe, conservative

3 Immediate, short-term impact
4 Entertainment value/appeal

- "Beyond the Frame" – Advantages of Visual Arts:

  1 Innovative, daring
  2 "Trendy"
  3 Long duration/impact
  4 Marketing tie-up opportunities
  5 Potentially large audience

"Beyond the Frame" seemed particularly attractive to Amway Japan because it had become fashionable to visit museums for social as well as aesthetic reasons, particularly among younger people – a category which corresponded to Amway's distributor and consumer audiences. Their lively interest in all aspects of American culture would be another reason for them to want to see the exhibition and to associate its innovative impact with Amway's.

Good citizen programs

Amway is a people-oriented, community-minded company. By funding environmental and good citizen programmes all over the world, it believes it is giving something of value back to the people who have contributed to its success and to the countries which have welcomed it.

Before sponsoring a cause or encouraging its distributors to raise funds for a local project, Amway engages in a long evaluation process:

1 *Identification.* Is the sponsorship something with which Amway wishes to be identified? Does it enhance corporate credibility, and will it support the Amway method of business?

2 *Uniqueness.* The sponsorship ideally should be tailored uniquely to Amway's needs and objectives. Special features and modifications should enable the project to be identified as a unique Amway sponsorship.

3 *Objectives/benefits.* The sponsor must clearly define objectives and anticipated benefits. Why does Amway want to do this, and what does it hope to achieve? The following is a listing of logical objectives for Amway:

(a) To create a platform for establishing valuable contacts/allies among key target publics in a positive way not easily achieved through other means.
(b) To enhance public visibility.
(c) To instill pride and motivation in the organization among employees, distributors, suppliers and customers.
(d) To strengthen the company's position in the local community.

139

(e) To diminish criticism that the company only takes profits out of the market without putting anything into it.

(f) To develop a pool of long-term goodwill in the environment to soften the impact of "crises" and maximize the benefits of success.

4   *Exclusivity*. Is this something which will be just one of many and "lost in the crowd", or will Amway have exclusive rights and benefits?

5   *Target publics*. To whom is Amway directing its efforts? It is essential that all audiences Amway wishes to reach are clearly identified and that realistic goals for perceived benefits among each group be developed.

6   *Long-term benefits*. Is there significant potential for benefits far into the future? One way of ensuring this is to sponsor an activity over a number of years which provides a vehicle for ongoing positive PR. If not, will the sponsorship (and attendant benefits) be quickly forgotten?

7   *Distributor participation*. A most important element in the success of any Amway sponsorship must be the ability to tie in the distributor organization. Distributor support and participation is not only beneficial in stimulating a sense of pride, but it is a necessity in order to avoid confusion, ill will and

disharmony. Without distributor support, a sponsorship, no matter how good, will inevitably have limited impact.

To sum up the Amway sponsorship policy, one might say the company gives with the hope (and calculated probability) of receiving a great deal in return. But does this really make Amway less generous, less laudable than any individual who gives to others not only out of pure altruism but to receive in return an enhanced self-image?

Action speaks louder than words

Green for life   We live on a crowded planet with limited resources. Amway has committed itself to long-term environmental stewardship and is following a responsible plan of action, being committed to being "green for life":

- *Biodegradability* Amway cleaning products contain biodegradable surfactants.

- *Concentration* Concentrated products contribute less solid waste.

- *No animal testing* Safety review processes of Amway products do not involve the use of animals.

- *Recyclable packaging* When technically feasible, packaging is made from recyclable and recycled materials. For instance, many Amway products are packaged in bottles made from post-consumer resins.

- *On-site recycling* Amway's goal is to recycle 90% of the solid waste it generates.

- *Using recycled materials* Most Amway newsletters are printed on recycled papers.

Fostering awareness of environmental concerns Amway recent actions:

- ICEWALK, the International North Pole Expedition. In 1989 eight explorers from seven countries became the first team to walk to the North Pole.

- ICEWALK International Student Expedition. Twenty-two young people from 15 countries came to the Arctic to study its ecology and culture, and conduct scientific experiments.

- ICEWALK Educational Video Series. Amway produced a four-part environmental video series about ICEWALK and its student expedition.

- GLOBAL RELEAF. Amway was one of the first sponsors and participants in this American Forestry Association project to plant 100 million trees.

- MASTERS OF THE ARCTIC. Amway Environmental Foundation sponsored an international traveling exhibition of Inuit and circumpolar artworks to be shown in various museums across the world.

- GENOA EXPO '92. Amway was a major sponsor of the US Pavilion at the international exposition to commemorate the voyage of Christopher Columbus.

14

The Compassionate Capitalist

On October 5, 1992, I had the great pleasure of interviewing Rich DeVos, co-founder of the Amway Corporation.

You are 66 now. What would you like to accomplish next?

Rich DeVos: An orderly transition of the management of the company, with both professional management and our family involvement in a proper transfer of leadership and power.

This subject has been on the agenda for several years?

Rich DeVos: It will probably still be on for several years more. The question is whether others are qualified to take on the responsibility and whether the old guys are willing to get out of the way.

Why do "the old guys" have to move to the sidelines?

Rich DeVos: Because young people must be included, because of the energy of youth. You have to be prepared in the event your life is shortened. You must always have a backup for your job. That does not mean that we have to disappear. The operating role in a large company requires lots of good people. I will remain personally involved as long as I can, but not on a day-to-day operating basis. I would like to remain active in policy and in inspirational leadership.

What are the key factors of Amway's success?

Originally we had the unique idea of empowering individual people to own their own businesses. And we had the right timing. We started when a lot of people were looking for a way to be entrepreneurs. We were on the leading edge of the concept of free enterprise, at the very time when others thought socialism was the great way of the future. We won, so to speak, because the shift, not only in our business, but in the world, moved in the direction of free enterprise.

We became part of a whole new movement back to the free enterprise system worldwide when the breakdown of communism began to occur. We were talking about free enterprise when everybody else was talking about socialism. In the free enterprise system, we emphasize the value and the efforts of the individual. Socialism emphasizes the value of the State. Our whole business is geared to individual rights, not the State's rights.

Jay Van Andel and myself both pioneered the idea because we grew up believing that the best thing in the world was to own your own business. That was given to us by our parents. Jay's father was in business for himself, and my father always wanted to be in business for himself. They felt that gave the best opportunity and the greatest amount of freedom.

Does this mean that all the people who work for large companies and don't have the chance of owning their businesses are unhappy?

Rich DeVos: They may be happier! Some people are just not made to run their own business, and therefore are much happier working under a more restricted organizational structure. They can use their ideas and their spirit just as well there as others do in their own businesses. It is a matter of being free to use your talent wherever you are working. Most people who choose to work for a large company, and 10,000 of them work for us, use their ideas and their energy to improve the company they work for. So it is a two-way street.

Maybe they work for you but they are not satisfied with their job?

Rich DeVos: Well, they can leave any time they like! But some people just do not have the confidence or the spirit of adventure that others do. They are afraid to go out on their own and need the security of a more regular job.

What did you learn during the last 35 years?

Rich DeVos: You mean what would I change? I think the biggest mistake we made back then was hiring the wrong people. If I look at our major problems, I see that we hired some people who really were not big enough for the job we had given them. It was not their fault, it was our fault. Therefore the biggest challenge as you build a business is hiring the right people.

How would you describe the strengths and weaknesses of Amway?

Rich DeVos: A company is never perfectly managed. We are always trying to see how many things we can accomplish with people who are not perfect. None of us is perfect, and therefore the job of management is never done perfectly because it is carried out by imperfect people. So what you need is a tolerant group of people who accept the fact that no one of us is perfect and we have to get the job done even though none of us does it perfectly all the time. That means you have to build a business with compassion and understanding of the real condition of human beings. The miracle of a business is that it can function under those conditions. It can function making mistakes but with less than maximum efficiency. You must try to do it the best you can and this is how we tried to build Amway.

I will give you an example. Jay and myself have never used the words "I told you so." When something went wrong, we did not spend any time blaming each other, we would just sit down and say "What do we do to fix it?" We built on problem solving, not on placing blame.

It is so easy in life to spend your energy blaming or finding the fault instead of trying to fix the problem! I think that is one of the reasons that Jay and I have been able to work well together for so long. We would concentrate on fixing.

You have had problems with distributors who do not respect the rules.

Rich DeVos: Well, you must treat them as exceptions. Most of the distributors want to play by the rules. Even those who may violate the rules temporarily can usually be persuaded to go back to playing by the rules. There are always a few who just won't do it right, no matter what you say or do. So, what you have to do is just find a way to gradually push them out of the business. But you have to be tolerant. It's a matter of how you want to work with people. Don't get so locked into your thinking that, because a few people break the rules, you have to have another thousand rules which hamper the progress of all the rest! That is what the government does all the time: it tries to protect everybody from everybody, and pretty soon nobody has any freedom to be creative, or use his or her ideas to make things better. With so many laws with which you have to comply, you can't even start a business in some countries. That's because they cannot tolerate the fact that we have to work in a world with a lot of imperfect people.

That does not mean that you should not strive for perfection. We have been criticized because we did not discipline enough. But when a society gets busy policing its people, pretty soon all the creativity and all the energy for improving the country disappears.

Most of the people I've dealt with had different ideas from mine, sometimes, they were better. When you become intolerant, you think that everybody is better off living within the rules. But maybe sometimes the rule is wrong. Maybe it is too restrictive. I think sometimes the government and lawyers, so busy arguing over little technicalities of the law, destroy the strength of mankind. That is certainly what happened with communism.

Today, after 35 years, Amway is still being criticized or misunderstood.

Rich DeVos: I consider that most of the critics are people who never built a business, never had a good idea or a new idea and spend their whole existence on the negative side of life. Therefore, they become intolerant of other people. Our critics are the kind of people who say we should ban all automobiles, because some people are killed in them. No one should be allowed to drive or to fly because it is not perfect. But we cannot stop the whole line of progress because it does not work perfectly.

The Amway opportunity is a trade-off. I have no restriction over the people who enter the business. Anybody can come in. I do not care if you have a police record. We do not bother to check on that. And therefore I get a bad apple once in a while. But if I start with all sorts of restrictions, I deny an opportunity to most of the people. I prefer my trade-off. I'd rather make sure that my opportunity is offered to everybody and take in a few bad apples. I'd rather keep my doors open and take my chances on cleaning house after a while.

Is this what you call "compassionate capitalism"?

Rich DeVos: I like to think of it as that. My book centers around that idea. I started to write the book because, like everybody, I watched the collapse of communism and socialism around the world and the emergence of free enterprise or capitalism. I believe unless capitalism has compassion, unless it is giving, caring, it will not survive either.

If you have an opportunity to make money thanks to other people, then you also have a responsibility to treat those people with love and compassion. You can't turn your back on those people. I have my profit, now what can I do to help you with yours? We have the responsibility to help people who are unable to help themselves. We have to understand the Christian foundation of capitalism, the way it began. It began with an attempt to improve the well-being of working people. It started out to try to help people live better and have a better income. I do not believe that the rich get richer and the poor get poorer, I believe that when the rich get richer, the poor must have a chance to get richer too. Our way of doing business gives the opportunity to make money to the new distributor, not only the old ones. That is the complete opposite of the pyramid scheme idea.

The pyramid scheme always says that the people at the top get it all. If you really understand the Amway plan, you realize it does not work that way. It gives an equal opportunity to the newest distributor and to the old. That is why our plan works when so many others fail. So many other companies never understand that principle.

Why do some people still have difficulty understanding Amway's philosophy?

Rich DeVos: People confuse Amway with other companies which try to imitate it. All the multi-level companies who try to copy us always try for shortcuts. They are not willing to make the efforts we made to build this business. They want a quick return on their money and they do not understand the philosophy or the principles of this business.

There is a whole spirit behind this business, allowing compassion. Our uniqueness is in empowering the individual. Most companies are like most governments: they like control. Controlling people is only secondary, after giving them the opportunity. But most companies are more interested in control than they are in the opportunities for the individuals.

Why is control so attractive?

Rich DeVos: People do not trust other people. In many companies you have layers of supervisors and under-supervisors who control the work of other people. Everybody watches everybody. At Amway, each month we pay millions of cheques for bonuses. People do trust this company.

Will your business philosophy be accepted in countries like China or those of the former Soviet Union?

Rich DeVos: Those people have been dominated during all their history. It is a question of mentality. They will need a generation to change their attitude.

Are you today as optimistic about the future as you were 35 years ago?

Rich DeVos: Look at what happened during the last 30 years. I was optimistic 30 years ago when everybody thought communism was on the rise. Russia was moving all over the world killing people by the millions. So was China in those days. You can't help being optimistic when you look at the relative peace throughout the world. We are all driving better cars, we are doing more things to help those places in the world where people don't have enough to eat. There are a lot of wonderful things going on.

So your optimism is not only about Amway, but about this world?

Rich DeVos: Absolutely, I grew up during world war II! How could I not appreciate how good we have it today! You've got to put things in perspective once in a while!

How do you explain the fact that so many people are not optimistic but, sometimes, feel depressed or discouraged about the future?

Rich DeVos: Maybe because jealousy today is dominant. Envy. Because of instant communication we see other people living better than we do and therefore we make ourselves unhappy over it. In the old days, we lived in a small community, and we were all poor but we were all happy together. And we all figured we could do better. If we had a measure of hope . . . . If we got an education and worked hard. Today a lot of people have given up those ideas.

The Amway message is one of hope: you can do better, you will do better and life will be better for you and your children. Maybe it is because the press writes so much about the few people who are not doing well, and forgets to write about all the good people who are doing well. In the United States, we have seven percent unemployment, which means 93 percent of our people go to work everyday. But all the noise is about the unemployed.

In the United States, will Amway develop as much as in the past?

Rich DeVos: In 1992, we are up 30 percent. We have more people joining Amway here than we ever had. All the people who were laughing at us only five years ago are not laughing any more. They are getting into the business today.

There are more and more people who are beginning to be amazed at how well we have done. I have seen tremendous changes during the last two or three years. Even the comics who used to make fun of Amway on television do it in a different way now. It's now a sort of grudging respect, not ridicule, and we do not get much negative newspaper coverage here any more.

How will you solve the problem of passing the responsibility to the next generation?

Rich DeVos: In the first place, all our children are not equally interested in pursuing the business. Why should they be? Just because they happen to be our children does not mean that they are interested in the business. They may have some other interests: the arts, politics, something else. They have the right to do what they want with their lives. They have all sorts of opportunities for public service. They can engage themselves and use their talents in different ways within the business. They will always be the caretakers of it, and undoubtedly the general owners of it. But they do not have to be the managers on a day-to-day basis.

Some of them may not yet know exactly what they want to do?

Rich DeVos: Neither did I when I started. Today, some of them may not be interested or qualified and a year from now they may be very much interested and very much qualified. And they may come to that point by doing other things.

Will the ones who take over have to make a life commitment?

Rich DeVos: That's correct. But we have to find out which ones want to and have the instinct for it.

It may take another several years

Rich DeVos: Yes. That is the process. In the meantime,

there are others who run the business day-to-day but all the children have exercised the responsibility of policy-setting and protection of the distributors rights. That is their main concern today.

How do you see Amway in the year 2000?

Rich DeVos: I see it as three times bigger than today: a $10 billion business with five million families of distributors operating in some 75 or 80 countries.

Box 6: AMWAY CO-FOUNDER RICH DEVOS AN-NOUNCES RETIREMENT: DICK DEVOS NAMED TO SUCCEED HIM AS PRESIDENT

Ada, Mich., Dec. 21, 1992 – Amway Co-founder Richard M. DeVos today announced his retirement as President of the global direct sales corporation and, along with partner Jay Van Andel, named eldest son Dick DeVos as his successor.

Tom Eggleston, Amway's newly appointed Chief Operating Officer and Executive Vice President for worldwide direct sales, said the appointment will ensure that the legacy of Rich DeVos will continue. "Rich DeVos is irreplaceable and will be missed as President by all of our employees and distributors," he said. "But we're very fortunate to have Dick, with his proven leadership skill, as our new president. I look forward to working with him in his new position. I know he shares his father's successful business philosophy."

Dick DeVos, 37, said that while his father will not continue day-to-day Amway responsibilities, as company co-founder his presence at Amway will remain.

The succession of a second-generation family member to the office of President closely follows the announcement in June this year of the formation of the Amway Policy Board. Policy Board, the top decision-making body at Amway, is comprised of Rich DeVos and Jay Van Andel, along with their family members: Dick DeVos; Dan DeVos, 34; Cheri DeVos Vander Weide, 31; Doug DeVos, 28; Nan Van Andel, 39; Steve Van Andel, 37; Dave Van Andel, 33; and Barb Van Andel-Gaby, 30. Policy Board activities are coordinated through a four-member Executive Committee: Chairman Steve Van Andel, Dick DeVos, Dave Van Andel and Dan DeVos.

Beginning with the opening of an affiliate in Australia in 1971, Amway has been introducing its marketing method internationally.

For the fiscal year ended Aug. 31, 1992, Amway Corp. reported annual sales at an estimated retail of $3.9 billion, a 26 percent increase from the previous year. More than two million independent distributors in more than 50 countries and territories market products from Amway's line of 400 homecare, personal care, health and fitness, home tech, and commercial lines, another 5,000 brand-name items from the US PERSONAL SHOPPERS catalog, plus a variety of services and educational products. Amway has more than 10,000 employees worldwide.

15

The Year 2000

Rich DeVos envisions Amway in the year 2000 as a $10 billion business, present in at least 75 countries, with five million distributors worldwide. Is this unreasonable optimism or can Amway really expand that much that fast?

Taking into consideration its growth in 1991–2, its plans for 1994 (China is just one example) and its longer-range European plans, it is not inconceivable that Rich DeVos' vision will become a reality.

In 1991, Amway entered East Germany, Korea, Brazil and Hungary. In 1992, headquarters were opened in Portugal, Indonesia and Poland. In 1993, they opened in Argentina, and in 1994, Amway hopes to be present in the Republic of China. Entering three to four countries a year requires heavy investment. In 1991, Amway spent $200 million to support new growth, in 1992 it spent $250 million, including an initial investment of $29 million in the vast factory it will build in Guangdong Province, China.

Amway distributors and executives will long remember the fantastic growth in the early 1990s in Japan, Thailand, Hong Kong and Taiwan ... the 40,000 distributor applications received during Amway Mexico's first year of existence ... the 35,000 new applications received in three weeks in Hungary ... the German and Spanish "explosions." Stewart McArthur, head of European operations, recalled:

"In 1990, we recruited 70,000 new distributors. In 1991, 375,000. That year we offered 200 new products. Our staff expanded from 350 to 750 people across Europe. We issued 18 new catalogs for $80 million sales in 1992."

Sales outside the United States today account for 70 percent of Amway's total turnover, but sales and recruiting in the US were also on the rise in 1992, about 20 percent more than 1991. The recession and job uncertainty have played a part in the domestic surge. "When people are insecure in their jobs, they look for an alternative," says Rich DeVos. Increasingly, doctors, lawyers and teachers are using their spare time to sell some of the 5,000 products proposed in Amway catalogs.

By 1991, Amway was offering, in addition to the products it makes or commissions, a variety of brand-name products and services, such as Coca Cola dispensers, MCI telephone services, Sharp and Philips electronic products. This trend is developing fast as more and more major companies begin to appreciate Amway's formidable worldwide sales force. Enlarging market opportunities is just one element of the Amway strategy for achieving its goal of a $10 billion business by the year 2000.

Stewart McArthur outlined the 11 objectives of Amway Europe's strategy.

1   To generate for the shareholder an optimum profit return on sales and capital whilst ensuring necessary re-investments into the business are possible.

2   To progressively move the balance of business from wholesale to retail consumption and to measure improvement.

3   To develop a broad array of initiatives between company and leadership which will increase the fidelity of this key relationship.

4   The progressive commitment and understanding to a European-managed business, thus taking max-imum advantage of the process of the international market.

5   To improve the image and business positioning of the Amway sales and marketing programme, thus strengthening the foundation and aiding planning and investment.

6   To clearly become an organization dedicated to the quality of service to our customers.

7   To widen the marketing and distribution channels of opportunity available to us in line with our positioning as a broadly based marketer of products, services and benefits.

8 To create an atmosphere for staff and management in Europe which rewards efforts and commitment through just compensation packages, appropriate training and career opportunities.

9 To expand the Amway business into all countries in Europe where entry, however creatively, is possible.

10 To ensure environmental commitment through public relations and marketing platforms.

11 To establish adequate management infrastructure to support the evolving business.

These objectives, McArthur told me, "are the framework of support of our European business. We will reach them because we concentrate on service quality to our customers, and we emphasize teamworking, everybody forgetting about personal prominence for the good of the whole. We strive to break down all the barriers. Amway is an open and transparent company. We just lived the most incredible and successful years in Europe and the years ahead will be just as positive. We will be an increasingly respected player in the European arena."

I believe that, in the best of all possible worlds, the year 2000 will be a time of new thinking. More and more people, aware of the opportunity of free enterprise, will discover new ways to express themselves and grow.

All through this book, I have raised a number of questions for which I have no definite answers. But I think more and more companies will ask themselves these questions and find the answers, if they are to survive.

In the year 2000:

- Will aggressive competitiveness still be relevant or will sharing, transparency, and spontaneous confidence in others be the rule?

- Will having not only pleasure but real fun for professional life be the only way to succeed?

- Will mixing personal and business life be the most profitable solution?

- Should the constant search for improving communication, building and managing relationships be our primary goals?

- Since freedom is a basic need, but also a frightening experience, should we try to be more liberated or remain bound in our old ways of thinking and acting?

Are these questions too utopian or just common sense?

16

A Way of Thinking, a Way of Acting

Amway is 35 years old . . . and one of the youngest companies in the world. Innovative from the very start, it continues to be ahead of the times in its management, marketing and logistic and motivational methods, and, for this very reason, to be misunderstood. Self-renewing, permanently new, it is, like anything new, the object of skepticism and sometimes vehement criticism.

One might say, of course, that its founders were "looking for trouble" when they chose to function in the realm of direct selling, that black sheep of the commercial world. No country in the world trusts or respects the direct selling industry, in spite of its $45 billion turnover and its constantly accelerating growth. Certain exploitive, dishonest methods, practiced by an infinitesimal minority are often taken to be the rule of direct selling when, in fact, they are the exceptions. All over the world, legislators are no less confused than the general public. Many laws concerning direct marketing are imprecise or fluctuating, when they exist at all. But instead of accepting this ambiguous situation, Amway, with its authentic vocation for innovation, has instigated regulations. In this way, it has smoothed the way for itself . . . and also for its competitors.

Amway is young too because it is neither set in its ways nor heavy on its feet. Although it has become a vast multinational corporation, it has remained flexible, mobile and capable of making rapid changes in a rapidly changing world. One example: in the face of unpredictable events, the launch of a new market can be put off or, on the contrary, advanced by several months. Possible only when a company is organized for adaptability and when its staff and network are motivated enough to roll with the waves, such feats of suppleness will be more and more necessary in businesses that want to progress rapidly in the international marketplace.

Dedicated, persevering staff members, motivated distributors, satisfied customers . . . it is clear that enthusiastic people are what all successful multi-level marketing is about. At Amway, managers and distributors really seem to enjoy their work and also the training sessions, the social activities, the seminars and the rallies which have become such an important part of their life. Why are they so satisfied? Not only because they have well-paid jobs or are developing profitable businesses for themselves, but because they have learned to help other people succeed as well.

I mentioned at the beginning of this book that I am an educator. I realize now that one of the deepest satisfactions I find in my work is the same as Amway distributors find in theirs knowing that the people you have helped grow will one day help others who in turn will help others. As Rich DeVos understood over 35 years ago, this simple certitude can be one of the most rewarding things in life.

I have often wondered just what the cost of quality is in the Amway business. I know that there is no specific budget for quality and that no attempts have yet been made to develop circles of quality or other benchmarking activities, which is to say methods of comparison with competitors. But I have been witness to a permanent and constantly reaffirmed drive to improve every aspect of the business. I never met anyone at Amway who was content to rest on his laurels. All seem to share the deep conviction that they can do still better, even after more than 35 years' experience in the same field. This attitude reminds me of Bertelsmann's, of Readers Digest's and that of Time Life Books, communication specialists, like Amway, which use direct selling. Each of them, although immensely successful, has unceasingly continued to test, to innovate and to strive for perfection.

Perhaps the most remarkable quality of these leading service companies is their capacity to motivate their personnel and all their collaborators, to energize them and inspire them not only to face change but to generate it.

Setting a good example

Just about everybody would like to be inspired and motivated by a strong and dependable role model. Rich DeVos and Jay Van Andel understood this earlier than most and acted on it more intensely. They have used the story of their own perseverence, their own originality, their own success and they have repeatedly expressed their own deep convictions to stimulate their staff and distributors, to help them grow and to realize their potential. With sincerity and simplicity they have set an excellent example their people are free to follow.

Other outstanding business leaders have understood that their personal example can be a major factor in the success of their companies. There is no doubt that the success of Bertelsmann throughout the world is largely due to the example set by Reinhardt Mohn. His rigorous management, his high standards of quality and also his determination to make his employees stock-owners of their own company have been powerful motivational tools. As for Luciano Benetton, his personal style is very different from Mohn's, but his example is an inspiration to a vast network of franchisees. Ingvar Kamprad, the founder of Ikea never tires of repeating his conviction: simplicity makes us strong.

Simplicity is a key word too for Rich DeVos. Every month for 30 years – some 360 times – his editorial written with Jay Van Andel on the first page of the *AMAGRAM* magazine has been sent to the homes of each and every Amway distributor throughout the world. Using straight-from-the-heart plain talk, he informs, advises, encourages or expresses his appreciation. He sounds sincere for the simple reason that he is sincere . . . and his distributors know it.

They know too that they were given an opportunity and that it was entirely up to them to take it or leave it. The respect of this freedom to try, to persevere, to succeed or, on the contrary, to turn away the challenge is at the heart of the Amway attitude of *detached involvement.* A key UK distributor once summarized this non-aggressive philosophy which takes into account human nature by the formula 3 sw. It refers to all potential distributors and means some will, some won't and . . . so what?

Rich DeVos and Jay Van Andel are now coming to the end of their active professional lives after having given millions of people the possibility to achieve their goals. Born in the land of opportunity, they have crossed border after border to create a world of opportunity. May their successors go farther still . . . in the same spirit of youth and freedom.

Bibliography of Recommended Reading

Barhan, Kevin and Oates, David 1991: *The International Manager*. London: The Economist Books.

Businesses everywhere are experimenting with new approaches cutting across national boundaries and allowing the most flexible use of corporate resources. But to make these work a new breed of manager must be in place, the type of person who can survive and even flourish in changing environments and cultures. K. Barhan and D. Oates describe who the international managers are, what kind of skills they need, how they can be trained and developed. They draw upon the experience of nearly 50 European, American and Japanese companies to produce a template for international management development.

Clothier, Peter 1990: *Multi-Level Marketing. A practical guide to successful network selling*. London: Kogan Page.

In an effort to dispel the myths – both good and bad – which surround multi-level marketing, Peter Clothier describes exactly what MLM is, the concept behind it, how it works in practice, and how to find the right opening. As an experienced trading standards officer, he writes about the business fairly and objectively. Stressing its high international standing, he explains how MLM is based on strictly commendable sales practices, and has nothing to do with pyramid selling. While emphasizing the need for personal commitment and enthusiasm, the book shows: how MLM differs from orthodox business methods; why MLM is a good way of selling a product or service and how it can quickly grow into a successful business; why starting such a business involves no significant risks; how to create an effective commission structure and bonus scheme; how and why market leaders are so successful; how to get started and the best ways of expanding the business.

Garfield, Charles 1992: Second to None. Homewood IL: Business One Irwin.

In an era of uncertainty the corporation, like any other social organism, is undergoing an extraordinary transformation in its attempt to operate in the global marketplace. The business leaders profiled in this book vary widely, but they all share a heartfelt commitment to reconciling the welfare of their people with their need for profits. It is not that they are unconcerned about the bottom line, but their humanism is pragmatic and results-oriented. They understand that profits are far more likely to be generated by employees who are treated with dignity and respect, in an environment that is a true community and not just a place to work.

Harris, Philip and Moran, Robert 1991: Managing Cultural Differences. Houston TX: Gulf Publishing.

Management is growing more and more aware of the influence of culture on employee behavior, customer relations, work, and productivity. Numbers of executives recognize that today learning for greater cultural understanding and competency must be an essential part of all management and professional development. Cross-cultural effectiveness is analyzed particularly in terms of the international assignment and technology transfer. Special attention is devoted to means and methods of human resource development, collaboration, and networking among professionals and technicians. The book contains many case studies, self-assessment tools and instruments for data-gathering and analysis.

Mole, John 1992: Mind Your Manners. London: Nicholas Brealey Publishing.

Managers working in a multicultural environment often make two mistakes; they misunderstand the behavioral and cultural differences, or are over-sensitive and defensive. Both can lead to reduced effectiveness and alienation – even confrontation. This book is a practical guide for the manager in Europe. It addresses the crucial issues of the legal and business framework, formal and informal meetings, social expectations, etiquette and manners. It is an effective tool aimed at managers of any nationality intending to do successful business in the single European market.

Normann, Richard 1991: Service Management. Strategy and leadership in service businesses. New York: John Wiley.

In the world of industry and management, the service industry is unique. This book provides a comprehensive framework on unique management issues and looks into the special characteristics of services and conditions necessary for success in the management of service organizations. The book stresses the need for a streamlined service management system and analyzes and illustrates growth strategies and the nature of innovation – particularly the nature of social innovation. But above all it emphasizes the special role played by good leadership. The use of image and culture as management instruments, effective and pervasive communication, and "high social technology" are explored and it is demonstrated how the "high social technology" are explored and it is demonstrated how the "new culture" of today's successful service organizations, if well implemented, can help achieve consistent quality of services.

Parikh, Jagdish 1991: Managing Your Self. Cambridge MA: Basil Blackwell Ltd.

With the help of this book anyone must be able to enjoy more effective, dynamic and fulfilling professional and personal lives. Better self-management increases managers' ability to cope with stress, manage change and manage to change, build and lead effective teams. As managers become increasingly exposed to new concepts and technologies, the gap between what they want to do and what they are actually able to do is growing. This book is an attempt to provide the missing link and it shows that successful corporations have a larger number of high performing individuals and that developing individual effectiveness is crucial for business success.

Peters, Tom 1992: Liberation Management. New York: Alfred A. Knopf.

Peters projects a very near future in which the business organization as we know it will no longer exist. "Markets are fragmenting. Product offerings are multiplying. All goods and services are becoming fashion goods." Peters says, citing a bushel of evidence like this 1991 headline: "IBM to start announcing its Fall line." In the new economy, most of the world's work will be done in semi-permanent networks of small project-oriented teams, each one an autonomous, entrepreneurial center of opportunity; where the necessity for speed and flexibility dooms to the dodo's fate the hierarchical management structures we and our ancestors grew up with. Corporations are subcontracting almost everything, and joining in temporary alliances of all sizes and shapes to do this or that. Careers are fast becoming portfolios of jobs, on or off small or large firms' payrolls.

Phillips, Nicola 1992: Managing International Teams. London: Pitman Publishing.

As business becomes more global, international teams are becoming a feature of an increasing number of companies. Human resources are therefore characterized by a greater cultural contrast. This book provides a practical discussion of the cultural issues raised by increased globalization; the effect of different national cultures on management styles; how to get the best out of staff in multinational teams.

Roddick, Anita 1992: Body and Soul. London: Vermilion.

The story of The Body Shop – created in Great Britain in 1976 – by its founder, a woman who knew nothing about the business world and now manages an international corporation with 600 shops in 38 countries. Writes Anita Roddick: "One of our main responsibilities is to allow our employees to grow, to give them a chance of fulfilling themselves and enhancing the world around them. Nevertheless, we still have within our company many people who believe that working for an honourable employer and doing a good job day's pay is enough. It is not. It negates the mutual responsibilities of the employer and the employee: I educate you, you educate me; I help you, you help me; together we help others. We want our employees to be empowered to make their voices heard in the running of the company, to be involved in everything we do."

Senge, Peter 1990: The Fifth Discipline: the Art and Practice of the Learning Organization. New York: Doubleday.

The learning organization manages to avoid certain crippling disabilities that plague other organizations. The most serious is the delusion of learning from experience. We can no longer understand the future by relying on the past. To do so is to find ourselves trying to resolve the same problems over and over again, despite a changed context. P. Senge stresses that managers must give up their fixation on isolated events and focus on the underlying processes that impact the organization – processes to which we are "90 percent blind." "Learning disabilities are tragic in children, but they are fatal in organizations. Because of them, few corporations live even half as long as a person – most die before they reach the age of forty."

Whiteley, Richard 1992: The Customer Driven Company. Moving from Talk to Action. Reading MA: Addison-Wesley.

This book provides any manager in any size company with a proven, step-by-step program for implementing, measuring, and rewarding both the product and service excellence that leads to true customer loyalty. Dedicated to helping organizations improve quality and service, each chapter focuses on a cornerstone of the customer-driven company, offering dozens of creative ideas in case studies and analyses of quality leaders. Each ends with "Action Points" which managers should undertake to institute a customer-driven environment in their organization. These points take full shape in the unique Customer Focus Toolkit that rounds out the book. The Toolkit opens with a self-test, a vitally important diagnostic tool that determines where the organization is strong or weak, and where to begin implementing change. This is followed by a set of principles for developing a customer-focused vision.

Appendix 1

Amway Glossary of Terms

Amway satisfaction guarantee
If not satisfied with the product, the customer has the opportunity to return it for replacement, refund or credit toward a future purchase – no questions asked.

Business Volume (BV)
The term BV means Business Volume. These are the figures on which all bonuses are paid.

Buy-back rule
Amway's assurance that when a distributor leaves the business he or she will not be left holding an inventory of Amway product. The product will be bought back at distributor cost less a small handling fee.

Corporate sponsorship
A corporate project which benefits the local community, and/or society in general. Often focuses on the arts, sports events, the underprivileged, or the environment. The concept of

174

"corporate sponsorship" was initially generated in America and is quite unknown in some parts of the world. Amway is highly dedicated to this concept.

Direct selling industry
Amway is a member of this industry in which sales are transacted on a *direct* basis between seller and customer, outside a retail store environment.

Distributor
Independent business person who sells Amway product.

Downline
The one who is sponsored.

Fiscal year
September 1 through August 31.

International affiliate
Subsidiary of Amway in another country.

International sponsor
Distributor from another country who comes to a new market to sponsor new people into the Amway business.

Performance Bonus
The monthly payment of monies by Amway to Distributors determined by the value of the Distributor's purchase of Amway products in accordance with the Amway Sales and Marketing Plan.

Person-to-person marketing
Amway's particular way of describing its own approach of direct selling.

Point Value (PV)
Point Value is a figure given to each product. PV determines Performance Bonus percentage level each month (i.e. 3% to 21%).

Pyramid scheme
Many illegal pyramid schemes have given direct selling a bad reputation. An illegal pyramid is characterized by the requirement of high investment to enter, and the promise of money when others are recruited into the business. Rarely is product actually sold in an illegal pyramid scheme.

Rules of conduct
Guidelines which Amway distributors agree to follow, designed for consumer protection and preservation of the philosophy behind the Amway Sales Marketing Plan.

Sponsor/recruit
Invite new people to join the Amway business.

Starter kit
The packet of Amway informational literature and sometimes a few product samples which a new distributor must buy when joining the Amway business. This is the only investment necessary – usually a cost equivalent to approximately US$ 100 (product and literature).

Unauthorized pre-launch activity
Distributor sponsoring activities which may occur in a country prior to Amway's official launch. May jeopardize Amway's position in the new market – it is crucial to Amway to research and abide by any legal, tax, technical/regulatory process required by the government.

Upline
Sponsoring distributor.

Appendix 2

Action Learning in Self-renewing Organizations

To readers who may not have had the opportunity to work in organizations constructed as networks, the following quotes give key elements about those emerging companies.

These quotes reveal new values, new behavior, new perceptions about ways to conduct business. They have been selected from a wide range of thoughts from executives or employees of several firms, as well as educators or leaders in different fields of activity.

They relate to the way people behave or should behave in self-renewing organizations. Some may sound utopian. However more and more people seem to be able to make them a reality.

The reader can use them to audit the way he or she works, and relates to others in business life. They can also help to make him (or her) more aware of the frontiers that restrict them and can even lead to questions about their commitment to change.

We have two forms of reward in the world. One is recognition, and the other is dollars. We employ them both. (Rich DeVos)

It all goes to the same issue. How do you move power, knowledge, information, and rewards downward in an organization? (Edward Lawler)

Paradoxically, companies that focus on values instead of profits end up enhancing their profit picture as a result. (Charles Garfield)

The model of effectiveness: How the four key elements of an organization – work, people, the formal structure of a company, and the informal structure and process – fit together. (David Nadler)

Cultural chocs stimulate creativity. (Lindsay Owen-Jones)

We think of a company as a family. The employees and the management are in the same boat. It is a fate-sharing body. (Akio Morita)

Where there is agreement between father and son, the family will prosper. (Confucius)

Business does not have to be drudgery. It does not have to be the science of making money. It is something that people – employees, customers, suppliers, franchisees – can genuinely feel great about, but only on one condition: the company must never let itself become anything other than a human enterprise. (Anita Roddick)

Results are gained by exploiting opportunities, not by solving problems. (Peter Drucker)

Diversity does not help just the bottom line; it also

enables us to fulfill our potential, activates our creativity, liberates our talents, enriches our teams, and makes our organizations more fully human. (Charles Garfield)

Our values, our goals, our causes are every bit as valuable to us as our products and profits. (Anita Roddick)

They scream and yell for the same reason they do at a football game. They have discovered that it is fun to be around people who cheer other people on, who encourage people. (Rich DeVos)

Amway is a company which is interested in total quality of life for consumers, not just economic prosperity. (Peter Scacco)

The real difference between success and failure in a corporation can very often be traced to the question of how well the organization brings out the great energies and talents of its people. What does it do to help these people find common cause with each other? (Thomas Watson)

The purpose of an enterprise is to create and keep a customer. (Theodore Levitt)

A better everyday life means getting away from status and conventions. Being freer and more at ease as human beings. Simplicity in our behaviour gives us strength. (Ingvar Kamprad)

Chance favors the prepared mind. (Louis Pasteur)

Just because we are criticized overseas does not mean we have to shut up and take it. (Akio Morita)

The inability of bureaucratic organizations to be flexible and make good use of the energy, feelings and brain power of its people, forces companies to orient themselves towards new principles for management, organization and change.

The only sustainable competitve advantage for a company in a complex and turbulent environment is its capacity to learn and motivate people. (André Wierdsma)

Clearly the 1990s will provide a significant advantage to those companies who are able to resolve the paradox between organizational size and speed in the market-place. (Noel Tichy)

Six paradoxes of self-renewing organizations

A self-renewing company like Amway must enhance creativity but also supply the financial support and logistics for the rapid realization of innovations. It must be flexible and broad-minded but also seek to develop a high degree of expertise among professionals. It must encourage each manager to operate as a specialist *and* as a generalist. It must integrate the talents of technical experts and business leaders . . . . C.K. Cameron of Cambridge summarized the paradoxes of self-renewing organizations as follows:

1   *Loose/tight couplings.* To enhance creativity and innova-
    tion, leaders need to give people power throughout the

organization to initiate and sustain efforts based on the faith of an idea. Loose coupling fosters wide search and a creative perspective and allows individual units a fair degree of latitude. This autonomy must be coupled with sustained financial support and with tight coupling for quick execution of the innovation. This is the antithesis of the mechanistic system that drives many companies requiring multi-level approval for new projects which must show quick returns.

2 *High specialization and generalization of roles.* Innovation depends on professionals with a depth of expertise in their technical specialities. This frequently means they have been narrowly trained. At the same time they need to be flexible, broad-minded, and capable of working well with other professionals. They must blend the talents of technical experts and business leaders. Mechanistic systems product specialists and generalists but rarely do they nurture these qualities in the same person.

3 *Continuity/discontinuity of leadership.* New leadership brings a fresh perspective to an organization's stability and institutional memory. Both are needed. Change efforts require the sustained attention of a fairly stable group of highly committed leaders. Mechanistic organizations tend to miss this point and transfer managers in and out of units without regard to their commitment to a change mission.

4 *Productive conflict.* Conflict is a dual-edged sword. Unbridled it can bring out the worst in human nature resulting in violence and destruction. Properly channeled it is the source of energy for challenging people and renewing organizations. Organizations need both pro-

cesses that encourage contention and processes that foster consensus.

5 *Expanded and restricted search for information.* Organizations need to expand their ability to collect relevant information to enhance their problem-solving capacity. At the same time they must find ways to buffer decision makers from information overload. Analytic frameworks enable decision makers to reduce information and eliminate irrelevant data.

6 *The paradox of participation.* Democratic organizations are designed for a long term survival, not short-term gains. Survival in the 1990s depends on cooperation through involvement of the corporation's varied constituencies.

Appendix 3

Amway Affiliates and Branches

AMWAY OF AUSTRALIA PTY. LTD
46 Carrington Road
P.O. Box 202,
Castle Hill, NSW 2154,
Australia
Telephone number:
(61-2) 680-2222

AMWAY INTERNATIONAL, INC.-HONG KONG BRANCH
26/F Citicorp Centre
18 Whitfield Road,
Causeway Bay, Hong Kong
Telephone number:
(852) 566-2239

AMWAY MACAU LTD.
Rua de Pedro Coutinbo
Np. 52 Edificio Hio Fai,
Bloco D R/C, Macau
Telephone number:
(002) 853-527888

AMWAY JAPAN LTD.
Arco Tower,

1-8-1 Shimomeguro
Meguro-ku, Tokyo 153, Japan
Telephone number:
(81-3) 5434-8484

AMWAY KOREA LTD.
12th Floor, Dongsung Building
158-24 Samsung-dong,
Kangham-ku
Seoul, Korea 135-090
Telephone number:
(82-2) 556-6577

AMWAY (MALAYSIA) SDN. BHD.
No. 34 Jalan 223
46100 Petaling Jaya
Selangor, Malaysia
Telephone number:
(60-3) 755-5222

P.T. AMINDOWAY JAYA
(Indonesia Trading Company)
Wisma SSK – 2nd floor
JI. Daan Mogot Km 11
Jakarta 11460

184

Indonesia
Telephone number:
(62-21) 540-1428

P.T. AMWAY INDONESIA
(Indonesia Service Company)
Wisma SSK – 3rd floor
JI. Daan Mogot Km 11
Jakarta 11460
Indonesia
Telephone number:
(62-21) 540-2160

AMWAY OF NEW ZEALAND LIMITED
25 Springs Road,
East Tamaki, Auckland, New Zealand
Telephone number:
(64-9) 274-9494

AMWAY TAIWAN LIMITED
Central Commercial Bldg.
8th Floor, No. 18
Nanking E. Rd. Sec. 4,
Taipei, Taiwan
Telephone number:
886-2-741-7566

AMWAY (THAILAND) LTD.
52/183 Ramkhamhaeng Rd.
(Sukhapibal 3)
Huamark, Bangkapi
Bangkok 10240, Thailand
Telephone number:
(66-2) 374-8000

AMWAY CORPORATION
7575 Fulton Road E.
Ada, Michigan
U.S.A. 49355-0001
Telephone number:

(616) 676-6000

AMWAY OF CANADA, LTD.
3897 Exeter Rd.
P.O. Box 5706
London, Ontario N6A 4S5
Canada
Telephone number:
(519) 685-7700

AMWAY DE GUATEMALA, S.A.
7a Avenida 6-69, Zona 9
Guatemala City, Guatemala
Telephone number:
(502-2) 34-28-15

AMWAY DE MEXICO, S.A. DE C.V.
Washington 539 Ote., Piso 10
Monterrey, N.L.
Mexico, CP-64000
Telephone number:
(52-83) 19-80-00

AMWAY DE PANAMA, S.A.
Apartado 6-4200
El Dorado, Panama
Republic of Panama
Telephone number:
(507-61) 7676

AMWAY DO BRASIL LTD.
Av. Eng. Eusebio Stevaux 1257
04696 Sao Paulo-SP, Brazil
Telephone number:
(55-11) 548-2188

AMWAY GESELLSCHAFT M.B.H.
Wienerstrasse 720
A-2203 Grossebersdorf
Austria

185

Telephone number:
(43-2245) 5202

AMWAY BELGIUM CO.
Ikaroslaan 4
B-1930 Zaventem, Belgium
Telephone number:
(32-2) 720-5935

AMWAY (EUROPE) LTD
Bank House - 1st Floor
171 Midsummer Blvd.
Central Milton Keynes
MK9 1ED, England
Telephone number:
(44-908) 691118

AMWAY FRANCE S.A.R.L.
14 Avenue François Sommer
BP 140
F-92185 Antony CEDEX
France
Telephone number:
(33-1) 46-68-04-25

AMWAY GmbH
Benzstrasse 11-a-c
82178 Puchheim, Germany
Telephone number:
(49-89) 800940

AMWAY POLSKA, Sp. z o. o.
ul. Mangalia 4
02-758
Warsaw, Poland
Telephone number:
(48-2) 642-15-92

**AMWAY HUNGARIA
MARKETING, Kft.**
1089 Budapest
Kálvária tér 7, Hungary
Telephone number:

(36-1) 134-2988

AMWAY ITALIA s.r.l.
Via G. di Vittorio, 10
1-20094 Corsico (MI), Italy
Telephone number:
(39-2) 451-951

AMWAY NEDERLAND LTD.
Edisonstraat 18, Postbus 278
4000 AG Tiel, Netherlands
Telephone number:
(31-3440) 18344

AMWAY DE ESPANA, S.A.
C/Industria, 101-115
Poligono Gran Via, Zona 22A
08908 Hospitalet De Llobregat
Barcelona, Spain
Telephone number:
(34-3) 263-31-88

AMWAY PORTUGAL S.A.
Av. do Forte, 10, Carnaxide
2795 Linda-A-Velha
Portugal
Telephone number:
(351-1) 417-2890

**AMWAY (SWITZERLAND)
INC.**
Industriestrasse 444
4703 Kestenholz
Switzerland
Telephone number:
(41-62) 632-525

AMWAY (U.K.) LTD.
Snowdon Drive, Winterhill
Milton Keynes MK6 1AR
England
Telephone number:
(44-908) 679888

AMWAY ARGENTINA INC.
Maipu 939-P.B.
1006 Buenos Aires
Argentina
Telephone number:
(54-1) 312-7591

Countries and Territories Where Amway Operates

Anguilla	Grenada
Antigua	Guam
Argentina	Guatemala
Australia	Guernsey
Austria	Haiti
Azores	Hong Kong
Bahamas	Hungary
Barbados	Indonesia
Belgium	Republic of Ireland
Bermuda	Italy
Brazil	Japan
British Virgin Islands	Jersey
Brunei	Korea
Canada	Macau
Canary Islands	Madeira
Cayman Islands	Malaysia
Channel Islands	Mexico
Dominica	Monserrat
Dominican Republic	The Netherlands
France	Netherlands Antilles
French Antilles	(Aruba, Bonaire, Curaçao,
(Martinique, Guadaloupe)	Dutch St. Martin, Saba,
French Guiana	St. Eustatius)
Germany	New Zealand

Panama
Poland
Portugal
Puerto Rico
La Réunion
Spain
St. Kitts and Nevis
St. Lucia
St. Vincent
Switzerland
Taiwan (Republic of China)

Thailand
Trinidad and Tobago
Trust Territories of the
  Pacific (Mariana Islands,
  Marshall Islands, Caroline
  Islands)
Turks and Caicos Islands
United Kingdom
United States of America
U.S. Virgin Islands

Appendix 4

Amway Management (August, 1993)

Headquarters

President: *Dick DeVos*
Policy Board: *Co-founders and eight second generation members*
Executive Committee: *Dick DeVos, Dave Van Andel, Steve Van Andel, Dan DeVos*
Chief Operating Officer: *Tom Eggleston*
V.P. Human Resources: *Dwight Sawyer*
Sr. V.P. Operations: *Roger Beutner*
Sr. V.P. Market Development: *David Brenner*
Sr. V.P. Research and Development: *Greg Grochoski*
V.P. Catalog/Communications: *Nan Van Andel*
Dr. International Public Relations: *Peter Scacco*
V.P. Pacific: *Dan DeVos*
V.P. North American Sales: *Doug DeVos*
V.P. Corporate Affairs & Chairman – Executive Committee: *Steve Van Andel*
V.P. Worldwide Sales Plan Administration: *Bob Kerkstra*

West Pacific

Managing Director Australia, New Zealand: *Bruce Shankland*
Acting General Manager Australia: *Bill Duncan*
General Manager New Zealand: *Don Sutton*
President and Representative, Director Japan: *Richard Johnson*
Managing Director Hong Kong, Taiwan, China: *Eva Cheng*
General Manager Hong Kong: *Patrick Hau*
General Manager Taiwan: *Audie Wong*
General Manager Korea: *David Ussery*
Managing Director Malaysia, Thailand, Indonesia: *L.H. Choong*
General Manager Malaysia: *Han Kee Low*
General Manager Thailand: *Preecha Prakobkit*
General Manager Indonesia: *Peter Beaumont*

Latin America

Regional Manager Brazil, Mexico, Guatemala, Panama: *Russ Hall*
General Manager Argentina: *Steve Robbins*
General Manager Guatemala, Panama: *David Casanova*
General Manager Brazil: *Ken Smith*

Europe

Managing Director Europe: *Bruce Shankland*

Regional Managers

Austria, Hungary: *Klaus Tremmel*
Germany, Switzerland, Poland: *Jim Payne*

General Managers

Spain: *Dan Shuster*
France: *Nicolas Lefranc*
Italy: *Martine Heines*
United Kingdom:
Poland: *Marek Kulesza*
Portugal: *Luis Delgado*
Belgium/Netherlands: *Arie Van Vugt*

Appendix 5

Amway Product Groups*
US Market

* AMWAY and names in upper case type are trademarks of Amway Corporation, Ada, MI, USA; NUTRILITE, POSITRIM, ACTIVE 8 and NUTRIPET are trademarks of Nutrilite Products Inc., Buena Park, CA, USA.

Home care

Laundry products

1 TWIN POWER Phosphate Free Detergent and Fabric Softener
2 TWIN POWER Detergent and Fabric Softener
3 SA8 Plus Premium Laundry Concentrate
4 SA8 Liquid Detergent
5 KOOL WASH Gentle Liquid Detergent
6 AMWAY Improved Fabric Softener
7 SMASHING WHITE Laundry Booster
8 AMWAY Pre-Wash Laundry Liquid Soil & Stain Remover
9 AMWAY All Fabric Bleach
10 TRI-ZYME Laundry Pre-Soak and Detergent Booster
11 AMWAY Water Softening Compound
12 REDU Rust Stain Remover

Kitchen care

1 AMWAY Automatic Dishwasher Concentrate Soft Water Formula
2 CRYSTAL BRIGHT Automatic Dishwashing Formula
3 DISH DROPS Concentrated Dishwashing Liquid
4 SCRUB BUDS Stainless Steel Sponges
5 AMWAY Hard Water Film Remover
6 AMWAY Oven Cleaner Spray

Household cleaners

1 AMWAY Anti-Tarnish Silver Polish
2 AMWAY Metal Cleaner
3 AMWAY Chrome & Glass Cleaner
4 BUFF-UP Furniture Polish & Dust Control Spray
5 AMWAY Bowl Cleaner II
6 PURSUE Bowl Cleaner
7 BLUE POWER Automatic Toilet Bowl Cleaner
8 L.O.C. Liquid Organic Cleaner
9 L.O.C. Wall Mount Dispenser
10 ZOOM Spray Cleaner Concentrate
11 SEE SPRAY Window Cleaner Concentrate

Floor care

1 SUPER SWEEP Carpet Sweeper
2 AMWAY Rug Shampoo Applicator
3 MOP MATE Total Floor Care Formula
4 DURASHINE Floor Polish
5 MAGIC FOAM Spray Foam Carpet Cleaner

Air freshness

1 SCENTSCAPES Home Fragrance Sprays
2 SCENTSCAPES Potpourri
3 MOUNTAIN MIST Air Freshener
4 BORONIA Air Freshener
5 GREEN MEADOWS Air Freshener

Plant and garden care

1 **d-15** Insect Repellent Spray
2 AMWAY Quick-Killing Bug Spray
3 FIRST PRIZE Concentrated Plant Food
4 FIRST PRIZE Liquid Lawn Fertilizer

Apparel care

1 AMWAY Shoe Spray
2 REMOVE Fabric Spot Cleaner
3 **drifab** Water Repellent Spray

Car care

1 FREEDOM Synthetic Motor Oil
2 AMWAY Extra Oil Additive Concentrate
3 MINT CONDITION Car Care Products
4 WONDER MIST Silicone Lubricant and Rust Inhibitor

Health & beauty

Health & fitness

1 NUTRILITE Food Supplements
2 NUTRILITE Mineral Supplements
3 NUTRILITE Vitamin C Products
4 NUTRILITE Vitamin E Products
5 POSITRIM System for Weight Control
6 SNACK SENSE Snack Products
7 NUTRILITE Nutritious Drinks
8 NUTRIPET Pet Supplement
9 ACTIVE 8 Drink Mix Products

Personal care

1 ARTISTRY Cosmetics
2 ARTISTRY Skin Care Products
3 AMWAY LA COLLECTION or CLASSIQUE
   Fragrances

Family care

1 SATINIQUE Hair Care Products
2 NATURE SHOWER Bath and Body Products
3 AMWAY Travel Organizer
4 DETER Deodorant and Anti-Perspirant Products
5 GLISTER Oral Care Products
6 SUN PACER Sun Care Products

Men's care

1 AMWAY GROOMING GEAR Products for Men

Home tech

Housewares

1 AMWAY QUEEN Cookware
2 AMWAY THE COMPATIBLES Housewares

Home environment products

1 AMWAY Water Treatment System
2 AMGARD Security Alarm Systems

Services

1 AMWAY Motoring Plan
2 AMWAY/MCI Residential and Commercial Service
3 AMVOX by Voice-Tel Telephone Messaging Service
4 Atlas Van Lines
5 Visa Credit Card

Commercial

Laundry products

1 SA8 Laundry Products
2 AMWAY All Fabric Bleach
3 AMWAY Fabric Softener & Brightener
4 TRI-ZYME Pre-soak and Detergent Booster
5 SMASHING WHITE Laundry Booster

Janitorial products

1 LEADOFF Floor Sealer
2 DURASHINE Floor Polish
3 POWER OFF Heavy-Duty Stripper Concentrate
4 INDUSTROCLEAN Heavy-Duty Cleaner

Agricultural products

1 APSA-80 All Purpose Spray Adjuvant Concentrated
2 AMWAY Defoamer

Food service

1 DISH DROPS Concentrated Dishwashing Compound
2 AMWAY Automatic Dishwashing Liquid

Appendix 6

Some Amway publications

AMAGRAM Magazine

Audience. All Amway distributors. This magazine is Amway's primary publication and often Amway's only communication link to small-volume distributors.

Objective. To inform, recognize and motivate the distributor organization and to promote Amway products.

Timetable. Introduction of the *AMAGRAM* magazine coincides with the launch of Amway into the marketplace, with new affiliates often producing every other month until their markets can bear the cost of monthly printing. Eventually, each affiliate will produce 12 issues a year.

Content. Each issue provides a mixture of professional photography and copy highlighting distributor recognition, product merchandising tips, new product information, product advertisements, distributor events, and general information and procedures concerning the Amway distributor business.

Cost. Generally, each distributor automatically receives a subscription to *Amagram* and continues to receive copies until the distributorship no longer renews.

Newsgram

Audience. Direct Distributors and above who, because of their distributorship level, serve as leaders within their organization.

Objective. Provides timely, pertinent and up-to-date information to distributor leaders that will help them effectively operate and manage their day-to-day business.

Timetable. Newsgram is introduced when the market has developed to the point that a second publication is cost-efficient and practical. Ideally, the *Newsgram* is published twice a month in a 2-color tabloid format.

Content. The subject matter covers a wide variety of topics, including:

- product availability
- price changes
- legal matters
- ordering procedures
- meeting announcements
- literature and sales aids
- promotional contests
- other crucial business information

Cost. Each affiliate supplies *Newsgram* either free of charge or through standing order subscriptions.

Diamond News

Audience. Diamond Direct Distributors and above.

Objective. Provides exclusive and advance notification of information that is pertinent to Amway's premier leadership.

Timetable. Diamond News is introduced when it becomes practical and efficient. It is published as often as once or twice a month, depending on the urgency and importance of news that needs to be forwarded to Amway's top producing distributors. Usually the bulletins are one page and printed on affiliate letterhead stationery.

Content. The subject matter in *Diamond News* varies widely. Among the topics are changing incentives, legal briefs, global and/or corporate information, new products and services, and Executive Diamond Council news.

Cost. Diamond News is supplied free of charge.

JUST AMONG FRIENDS Customer Magazine

Audience. Distributors and customers.

Objective. This 4-color publication is intended for distributors to leave behind with customers. The publication provides useful and valuable consumer tips in a casual and professional way, while generating an interest in AMWAY products. An underlying benefit of this "goodwill" publication is that it also promotes the Amway business opportunity to customers who are potential distributors.

Timetable. This periodic magazine is introduced when the affiliate is large enough to make it practical and cost efficient. Some affiliates have initially introduced *Just Among Friends* as a quarterly publication.

Content. A different theme is selected in each issue to provide useful and interesting consumer tips such as home decorating or cooking. The themes are reinforced with Amway product advertisements, promotions and feature articles.

Cost. Subscriptions are through standing order – in eaches, packs, or a customer mailing list.

Appendix 7

Amway Sales Figures (at Estimated Retail) (1960–1992)

1960: $ 500,000
1965: $ 35 million
1970: $ 120 million
1975: $ 250 million
1980: $ 1.1 billion
1985: $ 1.2 billion
1986: $ 1.3 billion
1987: $ 1.5 billion
1988: $ 1.8 billion
1989: $ 1.9 billion
1990: $ 2.2 billion
1991: $ 3.0 billion
1992: $ 3.9 billion

Appendix 8

Legitimate Direct Selling Companies and Pyramid Schemes

Legitimate Direct
Selling Companies

Low entry fee
Start-up fee for all ethical direct selling companies is generally low, primarily to cover training materials, sales aids or demonstration kits.

Wide range of quality products
The companies sell a wide range of quality products to the general public.

The bulk of the sales are on repeat sales from satisfied consumers.

Illegal Pyramid Schemes

High entry fee
Illegal pyramid schemes often disguise high entry fees as part of the price charged for required purchases of training, product inventory etc. These schemes make their profits primarily from recruiting.

Products of dubious value
Illegal pyramid schemes are frequently disguised to appear as legitimate direct selling companies. Such schemes are not interested in marketing the best products, but those which are

This is only possible because these companies spend millions on research and development to develop quality products.

of dubious value. Instead, money is made in typical pyramid fashion, from recruiting, with new participants being pushed to purchase high cost/large volume inventory when they sign up.

Consumer guarantee and buy-back policy
Many companies have a consumer satisfaction guarantee and a buy-back policy for participants. Dissatisfied users could exchange the products back for money or for an equivalent amount in other products.

No guarantee/buy-back policy
Illegal pyramid schemes will not buy back unsold inventory. Such schemes will collapse very quickly if there is this condition for re-purchase of goods.

Long-term business
These companies are interested in long-term business. In every country that they operate, this criterion is important because the companies have an obligation to participants who are small businessmen in their own rights.

Get-rich-quick shemes
Illegal pyramid schemes are get-rich quick schemes. The nature of the pyramid, in which large numbers of people at the bottom of the pyramid pay money to a few people at the top, clearly explains why the scheme cannot sustain itself for long.

Achievements recognized
Recognition of achievement is based on efforts. This means that a participant's income is commensurate with the efforts he/she puts into the business.

Positions can be purchased.

Quality products
Established companies depend on selling to consumers quality products which offer value for money in order to establish a market.

Illegal pyramid schemes are not concerned with repeat sales to users of the products. Profits are made on volume sales to new recruits who buy the products not because they are useful or attractively priced, but because they must buy them to participate in the scheme. As a result, new participants are stuck with products that are way below the market value in relation to the high entry fees. Should the pyramid scheme collapse, there is no way for the participants to recover their 'investments'.

Independent distributors
These companies build up networks of independent small business persons to sell products.

Fraud!
Promoters of an illegal pyramid scheme are engaging in fraud by knowingly deceiving participants in the schemes.

205

No inventory loading
They have strict Rules of Conduct which, among other things, forbids its participants to load up on inventory.

Inventory loading
Participants in illegal pyramid schemes have no choice but to indulge in inventory loading or high fees to participate.

Lawful
Direct selling is a popular method of retailing which is recognized as a lawful and legitimate business in many countries including the U.S.

Unlawful
Illegal pyramid schemes have been outlawed throughout the United States and many countries around the world.

Appendix 9

The Federal Trade Commission – Amway Case

Federal Trade Commission (FTC) of the US ruled that Amway is not a pyramid scheme

During the late 1960s and 1970s the FTC, among its many activities, undertook the investigation of a number of pyramid schemes, which had been a source of major consumer fraud in the United States. These investigations included such notorious pyramids as Ger-Ro-Mar, Holiday Magic and Koscot, and the FTC decisions against these schemes were major steps in cleaning up the pyramid problem in the US market. In fact, these decisions proved to be significant guides to US state legislatures in drafting pyramid prohibition laws.

For Amway, a formal complaint was filed against the company in 1975. The FTC/Amway case was heard in 1977, and the Administrative Law Judge gave his initial decision in 1978. The full Commission gave its final decision in 1979. The FTC ruled that Amway is not a pyramid scheme:

The Amway Sales and Marketing Plan is not a pyramid plan. In less than 20 years, Amway has built a substantial manufacturing company and an efficient distribution system, which has brought new products into the market, notably into the highly oligopolistic soap and detergents market. Consumers are benefited by this new source of supply, and have responded by remarkable brand loyalty to Amway products. (93 FTC 706)

In finding that Amway is not a pyramid scheme the FTC noted a number of important factors, as follows:

- There is no requirement to pay any kind of "headhunting fee" (i.e., entry fee).

- One does not have to buy a large amount of inventory to become a distributor.

- A sponsoring distributor earns nothing by the mere act of sponsoring.

- Inventory loading is prevented by Amway's "Buy-back rule."

- The Amway Sales and Marketing plan is based upon the distribution of goods to consumers.

In light of these factors, FTC drew the following conclusion:

Given these facts, the Amway plan is significantly different from the pyramid plans condemned in *Koscot*, *Ger-Ro-Mar*, and *Holiday Magic*. Specifically, the Amway Plan is not a plan where participants purchase the right to earn profits by recruiting other participants, who themselves are interested in recruitment fees rather than the sale of products. (93 FTC 716-717)

The FTC decision was a watershed in that it clearly vindicated the Amway Sales and Marketing Plan and provided a clear distinction between legitimate operations like Amway and unlawful pyramid schemes. The outcome of this meant that a major US federal agency, after thorough study, determined that Amway is an ethical and lawful business.

Index

Index

Index

Index

Index